Sea  ... Pets

Seahorse Complete Owner's Manual
Seahorse care, health, tank, costs and feeding.
by
Edward Eldington

Table of Contents

Chapter 1: Introduction

The seahorse is an extraordinary marine creature that is found in waters as varied as rivers such as the Thames Estuary in the UK, coastal lagoons in South Africa, the Pacific, the Mediterranean and the warm waters of the Bahamas.

These bony fish – yes, they are fish – live in waters where there is seaweed, coral, seagrass or other aquatic plants, as they need vegetation or similar structures to live in. They are poor swimmers and do better in more protected environments.

The seahorse gets its common name from its rather equine appearance, which is due to its long neck, the shape of its head and its upright or vertical swimming posture. It belongs to the genus *Hippocampus*: "hippo" in Greek means "horse" and "kampos" is a "sea monster".

Seahorses belong to the same family as pipefish and sea-dragons: Sygnathidae. This is derived from the Greek words "syn", which means "together", and "gnathus" meaning "jaw". These marine creatures have fused snouts and do not have mouths and jaws that can open and close.

There is extraordinary diversity in terms of species within the seahorse genus and this includes significant differences in size, with the largest seahorses reaching an astonishing 14 inches or 35 centimetres in length and the smallest not growing beyond a tiny 0.6 inches or approximately 1.5 centimetres.

This book will introduce you to these amazing fish by looking at the different species, discussing their appearance and biology, typical seahorse behaviour, their feeding requirements, and what makes these creatures appealing and fascinating.

It will also tell you what you need to know in order to decide whether or not this is the pet for you and, if it is, how to select your seahorse, what you need to buy before you bring it home, and how to take proper care of it.

The hobbyist also has to know what these fish need with regards to their environment. All the necessary equipment and water and other parameters are examined, as the quality of the water and the general environment have a crucial bearing on the health and happiness of seahorses.

Like all fish, the seahorse is unfortunately susceptible to a number of different types of bacterial, parasitic and fungal infestations. Anyone who is serious about having a marine tank needs to know what to look for and how to deal with common seahorse ailments.

This book also contains helpful information on their mating behaviour, spawning and caring for the hatchlings or fry for those who are interested in breeding one or more of the seahorse species.

Other areas of discussion are the fish and invertebrates that the seahorse gets on with. It's important to only combine species that are compatible with each other so that you don't have to deal with aggression and bullying between fish.

Please note that some of the information in this book is not specific to the seahorse but can be applied to all marine or saltwater aquarium fish. I hope that you find this book both useful and fun to read!

I have been keeping seahorses for over 15 years and I think they are simply adorable and fascinating. I hope my knowledge about these cuties will help you to look after your seahorses. Good luck!

Chapter 2: Seahorse basics

1) Seahorse overview

These unique fish are found in multiple locations around the world. While specific habitats vary, the majority of seahorse species make their home in temperate and tropical waters, including some river estuaries. Generally, seahorses are found in shallow water, but some can live as deep as 525 feet or 60 meters!

They also need sheltered places to live in, as they are very poor swimmers. This makes seaweed, seagrass, coral reefs, waterweed and even mangroves ideal, as all of them offer shelter and places where seahorses can anchor themselves. Seahorses are territorial and males stay about 1 meter or a little over 3 feet from their 'patch', while the females will range much further from home.

Species are found in the Atlantic around the Bahamas, off the coasts of Japan and Australia and the in Pacific along the coast from North to South America. There are also seahorses in the Mediterranean. Others live in the Thames River Estuary in the UK and various lagoons and river mouths on the southwestern coast of South Africa.

In addition to the wide range of habitats and locations, they are also found in numerous species. The exact number is still disputed, with some sources stating that there are 47 species and others indicating that there are in fact 54 recognised species. In either case, with such a large number of species comes a wonderful array of shapes, colours and sizes!

One of the most remarkable aspects of the seahorse is that it is the male that gives birth to the young.

2) *Life span or expectancy*

The life expectancy of seahorses in the wild is unknown. However, there is one case of a tagged seahorse that was monitored by researchers for 5.5 years.

In captivity, the lifespan is between 1.5 and 7 years, depending on the species, care and environment. There have been reports of some surviving 10 years in captivity. Generally, larger species live longer than smaller ones.

Like most living creatures, these fish have enemies. The primary predators are large fish, crabs, penguins, skates, rays and water birds. Their best defences against predation lie in their ability to camouflage themselves and the fact that they are not all that appetizing thanks to their spines and bony structure.

The main threat to these fish in the wild is human beings because the seahorse is exploited for the Asian medicine market, tourist trinkets, caught for the pet trade and affected by changes to water temperatures and loss of habitat.

3) *Seahorse anatomy*

Basics:

The seahorse is a bony fish or teleost, and the genus belongs to the class *Actinopterygii*.

Like all fish, the seahorse has a head, body, tail and fins. As with most, the two eyes are set on either side of the head, as are the nostrils or nares. They also have gills. However, that is where the similarities end!

They have a skeleton that consists of numerous bony plates. While they too have a swim bladder that aids with buoyancy, the seahorse swims upright, which is one of their distinguishing and unique characteristics.

Size:

Hardly surprisingly given the large number of species, there is a great variation in terms of size.

The Pygmy Seahorse is the smallest and only reaches the length of 1 inch or 2.5 centimetres. The largest species grow to 12 inches or 30.5 centimetres.

Head and neck:

The head and neck are also unique features. The head is equine or shaped like that of a horse and the neck is long, flexible and well defined.

The horse-like head ends in a long, thin snout, which they use to get at food in nooks in rocks or coral and through which food is sucked. Seahorses do not have teeth.

There is a small group of spines on the top of the head, which is called the coronet, as it looks crown-like.

Gills:

Another feature shared with other fish is the gills they use to breathe. However, unlike other fish, the opening to the gills is a small hole at the back of the head that is protected by a bony cover called an operculum.

A further difference is that seahorse gills are "tufted". Tufting is an astounding adaptation that makes up for the small size of the opening to the gills. The gills look like small balls of tissue, each of which is on top of small stems or filaments called lamellae.

These structures are rich with blood vessels, which allow gas – both oxygen and carbon dioxide – diffusion. The fact that there are large numbers of these specialised structures means that the surface area for the absorption of gasses is increased within a small space.

Eyes:

The eyes of the seahorse are far more like those of a chameleon than a fish! This applies to both the fact that the eye protrudes from the head and the way they move.

Like a chameleon, a seahorse can move and rotate each eye independently. This allows it to look forwards and backwards at the same time, which helps when looking or hunting for food. Their eyesight is also very good.

Body covering:

The seahorse has an exoskeleton and no scales. The body consists of hard, bony plates that are fused together. They have thin skin that covers the exoskeleton through which the plates are visible and look like rings. Some species grow spines, bony protrusions or even filaments made of skin.

Fins:

Seahorses have dorsal and pectoral fins but no caudal fins. In addition to absent or very small fins, their body shape means that these fish are very poor or weak swimmers.

The dorsal fin on the back beats at an astonishing 30 to 70 times a minute and it is this fin that moves the seahorse through the water. The pectoral fins are very small and located on either side of the head. These little fins help with manoeuvring and stability.

Tail:

The seahorse's tail is entirely unlike the usual fish tail because it is a fairly long tail and tapers to a point. It is not like a fan at all. Furthermore, the tail plays no part in swimming as it does with other fish.

Most importantly, their tail is prehensile. This allows the seahorse to grasp onto seaweed, coral, grasses etc. and anchor itself in place. This is especially useful in light of its poor swimming ability.

Ability to change colour and shape:

Like several other marine creatures and the chameleon, seahorses are able to very rapidly change colour.

One purpose of changing colour is to become camouflaged and blend in with the environment. Other times that a seahorse will change colour is during courtship and when mating pairs greet each other.

The second astonishing aspect of camouflage is the ability some species have to grow spikes, filaments or bumps on or from their skin. These skin growths are normal and are called cirri. The purpose of them is for camouflage, which helps to keep them safe as they blend into their territory and the vegetation in it.

Gender:

Immature seahorses all look like females but mature male and female seahorses have several physical differences, which makes identifying the sexes fairly easy. Several of these differences are linked to reproductive organs.

Males have a "D" shaped body and a longer tail in proportion to the trunk or body than the female does. They also have a ridge, called the keel, running along the ventral side or front of the body. Perhaps the most notable gender difference is the brood pouch at the base of the tail. This pouch gives their tummies the more rounded shape.

Females, on the other hand, have no brood pouch or keel and in most species the snout is longer than the males. This difference in snout length is not great so it can be harder to use as a differentiation factor. The female body shape is more like a "P".

4) The history of the seahorse as a pet

According to Amanda Vincent in her article for *Natural History* in December 1990, seahorses were written about by the Roman natural historian Pliny the Elder and in *Gentleman's Magazine* in 1753. In both cases the seahorse was discussed in relation to the health benefits it offers.

It is not clear at all when seahorses began to appear in aquariums and tanks and began to form part of the marine and pet trades.

5) Types of Seahorse

There is disagreement about the number of seahorse species, but an alphabetical list published in 2012 recognised the following:

- *Hippocampus abdominalis* / big-belly seahorse
- *Hippocampus alatus* / winged seahorse
- *Hippocampus algiricus* / West African seahorse
- *Hippocampus angustus* / narrow-bellied seahorse
- *Hippocampus barbouri* / Barbour's seahorse
- *Hippocampus bargibanti* / pygmy seahorse
- *Hippocampus biocellatus* / false-eyed seahorse
- *Hippocampus borboniensis* / Réunion seahorse
- *Hippocampus breviceps* / short-headed seahorse
- *Hippocampus camelopardalis* / giraffe seahorse
- *Hippocampus capensis* / Knysna seahorse
- *Hippocampus colemani*
- *Hippocampus comes* / tiger-tail seahorse
- *Hippocampus coronatus* / crowned seahorse
- *Hippocampus curvicuspis* / New Caledonian thorny seahorse
- *Hippocampus debelius* / softcoral seahorse
- *Hippocampus denise* / Denise's pygmy seahorse
- *Hippocampus erectus* / lined seahorse
- *Hippocampus fisheri* / Fisher's seahorse
- *Hippocampus fuscus* / sea pony
- *Hippocampus grandiceps* / big-head seahorse
- *Hippocampus guttulatus* / long-snouted seahorse

- *Hippocampus hendriki* / eastern spiny seahorse
- *Hippocampus hippocampus* / short-snouted seahorse
- *Hippocampus histrix* / spiny seahorse
- *Hippocampus ingens* / Pacific seahorse
- *Hippocampus jayakari* / Jayakar's seahorse
- *Hippocampus jugumus* / collared seahorse
- *Hippocampus kelloggi* / great seahorse
- *Hippocampus kuda* / spotted seahorse
- *Hippocampus lichtensteinii* / Lichtenstein's seahorse
- *Hippocampus minotaur* / bullneck seahorse
- *Hippocampus mohnikei* / Japanese seahorse
- *Hippocampus montebelloensis* / Monte Bello seahorse
- *Hippocampus multispinus* / northern spiny seahorse
- *Hippocampus paradoxus* / paradoxical seahorse
- *Hippocampus patagonicus*
- *Hippocampus pontohi*
- *Hippocampus procerus* / high-crown seahorse
- *Hippocampus* / pygmy thorny seahorse
- *Hippocampus queenslandicus* / Queensland seahorse
- *Hippocampus reidi* / longsnout seahorse
- *Hippocampus satomiae* / Satomi's pygmy seahorse
- *Hippocampus semispinosus* / half-spined seahorse
- *Hippocampus severnsi*
- *Hippocampus sindonis* / Dhiho's seahorse
- *Hippocampus spinosissimus* / hedgehog seahorse
- *Hippocampus subelongatus* / West Australian seahorse
- *Hippocampus trimaculatus* / longnose seahorse
- *Hippocampus tyro*
- *Hippocampus waleananus* / Walea pygmy seahorse
- *Hippocampus whitei* / White's seahorse
- *Hippocampus zebra* / zebra seahorse
- *Hippocampus zosterae* / dwarf seahorse.

The various species differ primarily in terms of where they are found, the types of water they live in, their size, colour and the types of camouflage cirri they develop based on where they live.

6) Choosing the right seahorse species

There are some seahorses that are recommended for beginners as they are easier to care for and hardier than others. It must be noted, though, that seahorses are not as easy to look after as other fish found in tanks and aquariums.

In addition to species, there are other considerations that must be kept in mind. It is always, always far better to buy a captive bred seahorse from a reputable breeder, regardless of the species!

Suitable species for beginner aquarists

The species that are ideal for beginners are:

- ✓ *Hippocampus reidi* / **Brazilian Seahorse**: These larger fish grow to about 20 centimetres or 8 inches and are fairly easy to care for. Another reason they are popular is that they are found in bright colours such as red, orange and yellow in addition to grey, black and white.

  However, they are not a good choice if you want to breed seahorses, as this is not easy with this species. The other drawback is that wild caught adults are sold worldwide. These specimens should be avoided.

  A pair of these seahorses require a 30 gallon or 114 litre tank with a water temperature range of $21 - 23°$ Celsius or $70 - 74°$ Fahrenheit.

- ✓ *Hippocampus erectus* / **Lined Seahorse**: This species is perhaps the easiest to care for and therefore a good choice for a beginner aquarist. They reach approximately 20 centimetres or 8 inches in length.

  Apart from ease of feeding and being more disease resistant than many, the Lined Seahorse is often described as outgoing, active and social.

  They will also take on the predominant colour in their environment, so the tank owner can determine colour by selecting the colour of tank décor! This means they have the widest range of colours of any species in captivity.

They are also easier, although not easy, to breed.

A pair of Lined Seahorses need a 30 gallon or 114 litre tank with a water temperature range of 20 – 22° Celsius or 68 – 72° Fahrenheit.

✓ *Hippocampus kuda* / **Yellow Seahorse**: These are medium sized seahorses, as they grow to 15 centimetres or 6 inches. The name is a little misleading as these fish are also found in browns, creams and greys.

In terms of personality, they are a shy species that may even need encouragement to eat and tend to hide away. This makes them less easy to care for than the Lined and Brazilian Seahorse. They are easy to breed, however.

This species also requires a 30 gallon or 114 litre tank with a water temperature range of 21 – 23° Celsius or 70 – 74° Fahrenheit.

✓ *Hippocampus fuscus* / **Sea Pony**: These seahorses are smaller at only 5 inches or 12.5 centimetres. These are fairly inactive fish and they aren't especially colourful either (either bright yellow or black).

This is not a difficult species to breed or to care for. Because of their size, they also require a slightly smaller tank (20 gallons or 76 litres for a pair).

✓ *Hippocampus taeniopterus* / **Yellow Seahorse**: It is confusing that two separate species, *H. kuda* and *H. taeniopterus*, are called the Yellow Seahorse. There is debate over whether they are distinct species. However, several researchers believe that differences of colour and behaviour, particularly in the young, show that they are separate species.

These are also large seahorses as they grow to about 20 centimetres or 8 inches. Like *H. reidi* they are active and social seahorses that are easy to care for. Breeding is difficult, however.

There is little variation in colour with this species as they are usually all yellow, yellow with black, yellow with white, all black or yellow with orange dots.

A pair of seahorses needs a 30 gallon or 114 litre tank with a water temperature range of $21 - 23^\circ$ Celsius or $70 - 74^\circ$ Fahrenheit.

✓ *Hippocampus comes* / **Tiger Tail Seahorse**: This species is delicate-looking despite its size (7 inches or 18 centimetres) and it is characterised by a thin snout, small coronet, fine features and the striped tail that gives it its name.

The characteristic colour is yellow and black but others range from black to white with cream and yellows in between. When the stripes are clear and the colours are vibrant this is one of the most lovely seahorse species.

They are unfortunately very shy and cautious and will hide when the aquarist is near the tank. They are not as easy to care for as the species discussed previously and breeding them is very challenging.

This species also needs a 30 gallon or 114 litre tank with a water temperature range of $21 - 23^\circ$ Celsius or $70 - 74^\circ$ Fahrenheit.

✓ *Hippocampus zosterae* / **Dwarf Seahorse**: This species is the smallest, reaching only 1.5 inches or 3.8 centimetres. Overall they are not too hard to care for or to breed, but the tank must cater for their size.

A group of Dwarf Seahorses only needs 5 gallons or 19 litres of water in a tank. Not only do they not need much space, having a small tank makes it easier to feed them. However, one must be very careful that inlet and overflow pipes are the right size so that these small seahorses don't get hurt.

The primary challenge is that they can only eat live foods and they need to eat a great deal!

Water temperature should be in the $20 - 23^\circ$ Celsius or $68 - 74^\circ$ Fahrenheit range to keep these sweet little fish healthy.

More difficult species that are easily available

Some species are harder to feed and care for, which makes them a poor choice for an inexperienced aquarist. These species include:

✓ *Hippocampus barbouri* / **Zebra Snout Seahorse**: This is a popular species because these seahorses are very beautiful thanks to their bright colours (vibrant yellow, all white or bright orange) and striking striped faces. They grow to 6 inches or 15 centimetres.

Problems with the Zebra Snout Seahorse are that they are very difficult to care for, which means that mortality rates in captivity are fairly high. One reason for this is that they are not active feeders like most species and they also tend to be fussy eaters. Breeding this species is also hard.

A pair of Zebra Snout Seahorses need a 30 gallon or 114 litre tank with a water temperature range of $21 - 23^\circ$ Celsius or $70 - 74^\circ$ Fahrenheit.

✓ *Hippocampus ingens* / **Pacific Giant Seahorse**: As the name suggests, this is a large species as adults grow to 12 inches or 30 centimetres. They are found exclusively in subtropical waters.

They are found in appealing, bright colours: red, orange, and yellow in addition to grey, black and white. They are also active and outgoing, so they are not frightened of the aquarist and may even interact with him or her.

The downside is that the species is difficult to keep and is very susceptible to bacterial infections in particular. Breeding them is also hard. In addition, they can't be combined with other fish or seahorse species.

Because of their size, a pair of these seahorses requires a 50 gallon or 190 litre tank with a water temperature range of 20 – 23° Celsius or 68 – 74° Fahrenheit.

✓ *Hippocampus subelongatus* / **Tiger Snout Seahorse**: Like the Pacific Giant Seahorse, this species is from subtropical water, found in a range of attractive colours, is active and sociable and will interact with other seahorses and a human owner. They are slightly smaller than the *H. ingens,* at 20 centimetres or 8 inches.

However, they are difficult to care for and because many of these seahorses are wild-caught it can be a problem to get them to eat non-living foods. Like other wild caught creatures they can carry parasites and infections. Breeding is also very hard with this species.

A pair of these large seahorses will need a 40 gallon or 151 litre tank with a water temperature range of 20 – 22° Celsius or 68 – 72° Fahrenheit.

✓ *Hippocampus abdominalis* / **Pot Belly Seahorse**: These seahorses are active and sociable. They are the largest species and grow to 14 inches or 36 centimetres in length.

While they are difficult to care for, they breed very easily, don't form pair bonds and frequently give birth to very large broods! This species requires cool water and gets sick and dies quite quickly in water that is too warm.

This large species requires a big tank: 60 gallons or 227 litres of water with a temperature range of 13 – 18° Celsius or 55 – 65° Fahrenheit.

7) *Myths & misunderstandings about seahorses*

The seahorse is endangered

Some species are endangered, but the situation is complicated. With the majority of seahorse species there is not enough data or information to allow researchers and relevant bodies such as the International Union for Conservation of Nature (IUCN) to assess the status of a species.

The species that appear on the IUCN list as vulnerable species are the Three-Spot, Hedgehog, Great, Spotted, Spiny, Lined, Tiger Tail, Barbour's and West African Seahorse and the *H. planifrons*.

The only seahorse that appears on the IUCN Red List as endangered is the Knysna Seahorse. The reason for this is that their range is limited (3 coastal estuaries in South Africa) and the habitat is being affected by changes in water temperature, fishing activities and urban development. The Dwarf Seahorse may be added to the endangered list.

Shiho's Seahorse is the only species listed as "least concern".

The seahorse genus was added to the Convention on International Trade in Endangered Species (CITES) list in 2004 so an international treaty protects them. In effect, any countries that are signatories to this treaty are bound to protect any species on the list by regulating and controlling trade. However, this regulation often does not take place and seahorses are harvested by the million each year.

The specific threats to these fish are:

- The Asian, specifically Chinese, medicine trade is a huge threat to the seahorse; it is estimated that 150 million are captured and used each year!

- The pet or aquarium trade also poses a risk, as about 1 million specimens are caught and sold. Some believe that only about 10% of that number actually survives.

- A further million seahorses annually join the dried and bleached-looking starfish and seashells sold as souvenirs to tourists. They also end up as part of items such as paperweights, keychains and so forth.

- The destruction of seahorse habitats and changes in water temperatures are all threats to their survival.

- Finally, many seahorses are accidentally caught in fishing nets.

They are hard to care for

Unfortunately, this is accurate on the whole. However, as discussed, there are species that are less challenging and if the aquarist is prepared to learn about seahorse care, the specific species he or she has, and put in the necessary time and work, it can be done very successfully.

Those who have seahorses believe that keeping them is both worthwhile and addictive!

You need a license to keep seahorses

In most countries, there is no need for an aquarist or hobbyist to have a license to keep seahorses. If you are concerned, you can find out by contacting a reputable dealer or breeder in your area or one of the conservation bodies.

If you want to breed and sell seahorses across borders you will need to have the necessary paperwork. This usually includes the relevant CITES number or even a CITES certificate for exporting purposes.

They mate for life

This is an appealing, romantic thought but not true of the vast majority of seahorse species. What most species appear to do is to form bond pairs for a mating season.

This pair remains together and reinforces their bond daily but once the offspring are produced they go their separate ways.

Chapter 3: Seahorse behaviour

1) Social behaviour

Seahorses are a sedate, slow-moving species and they spend most of their lives feeding. Because they are weak swimmers, they spend a fair amount of time anchored to something by their tail rather than doing a great deal of free swimming.

They do have territories, which they stay quite close to. While seahorses are territorial, they are not aggressively so. Both males and females have ranges. The male's territory is usually 1 m^2 or approximately 11 square feet. The females have much larger ranges: 100 m^2 or approximately 1100 square feet.

The severe reduction in territory or range size when confined to a tank causes a great deal of stress, which leaves them vulnerable to illnesses that can in turn prove fatal. This is not the case for young seahorses bred in captivity, as they have never had a large territory.

While seahorses are generally placid, even shy creatures, they become more aggressive in restricted environments and may fight over females, food or territory. Their tails are their weapons during fights and they use them to grab their opponent. It is rather like wrestling and the combatants can get rather tangled but don't usually get badly hurt.

In addition to the courtship dance, which will be examined in a later chapter, a pair of seahorses will stay together for a mating season and greet each other each morning. Both seahorses float or rise together towards the surface of the water, quivering as they do. Other seahorses will swim side-by-side, with their tails twined together. The male may even appear to glow slightly.

Most of a seahorse's day consists of eating and remaining fairly stationary. So, if an active, entertaining pet is what you want the seahorse is not for you!

2) Compatibility with other fish species and marine life

Some aquarists believe that seahorses should be kept in species-specific tanks. In other words, one should only keep one seahorse species and there should be no other marine creatures in the tank with them. However, most tank owners do not subscribe to this view.

Seahorses are only territorial when it comes to competing for a mate, defending their territory or in the pursuit of food. Generally speaking, though, they are not aggressive; they are slow and docile creatures. They need tank mates with similar temperaments and behaviour patterns.

Fish that are a good combination with seahorses include the following species:

- ✓ Curious Worm fish
- ✓ Gobies (Bar, Neon, Shark-nose, Yellow Clown, Prawn, Black-finned / Watchman, Clown Shrimp, Rainford's, Yellow Eel, Scissortail and Blackray Shrimp Goby)
- ✓ Blue-Green Chromis
- ✓ Bluespotted, Yellowhead or Dusky Jawfish
- ✓ Most Blennies
- ✓ Firefish and Purple Firefish
- ✓ Green or Spotted Mandarin Fish
- ✓ Dragonet (Red Scooter, Scorpion or Scooter
- ✓ Cleaner, Sixline or Fourline Wrasse
- ✓ Leaf Fish
- ✓ False Percula Clownfish
- ✓ Cardinals
- ✓ Royal Gramma
- ✓ Dottyback.

Seahorses can also be placed with a range of marine invertebrates:

- ✓ Snails: Astraea, Cerith, Nassarius, Nerite, Turbo, Trochus,

- ✓ Starfish: Blue Linckia, Dotted Fromia, Marbled Fromia, Purple Linckia, Banded Serpent
- ✓ Fanworms and Feather Dusters
- ✓ Fighting and Queen Conch
- ✓ Lettuce Sea Slug
- ✓ Hermit Crabs: Blue-legged, Mexican Red-legged and Red Reef
- ✓ Crabs: Porcelain, Emerald, Arrow and Horseshoe
- ✓ Sponges
- ✓ Shrimp: Grass, Peppermint, Rockpool, Scarlet / Blood and Skunk Cleaner Shrimp.

Most corals are fine in a tank with seahorses. However, the general rule of thumb is that they should not be sharp-edged or have stings, as they are likely to injure the seahorses.

3) Compatibility with other seahorse species

This is a frequently discussed topic in seahorse website chatrooms and while the issue has still not been resolved, general consensus seems to be that combining different species of seahorse is not a good idea.

This is not because of any behavioural issues but because a species may introduce bacteria into the tank that it is immune to but that will infect and kill other species. One seahorse breeder likens the situation to the Spanish Conquistadors arriving in South America and infecting the local peoples with influenza, against which their immune systems had no defence.

4) What species the seahorse is incompatible with

Generally speaking seahorses get on well with other slow-moving and non-aggressive fish and with many invertebrates.

The fish they should not be housed with are:

- ▪ Other seahorse species

- Eels
- Groupers
- Sharks
- Trigger Fish
- Tangs.

The invertebrates that are *not* good tank mates are:

- Squid
- Cuttlefish
- Anemones
- Nautiluses
- Octopi
- Sea Cucumbers
- Lobsters
- Fire Worms
- Sea Urchins
- Nudibranchs
- Mantis Shrimp
- Some Flatworm species.

In other words, don't' combine seahorses with fast moving, large, or aggressive fish or other seahorse species. One should also avoid species that will compete with the seahorses for food.

Corals and invertebrates should not have sharp edges or stings, as these all pose a risk to the seahorses. For the sake of the tank owner, one should avoid corals etc. that have very specific requirements in terms of light and temperature.

It is necessary to ensure that the necessary tank and water parameters are compatible for all the species in the tank. For example, some corals require a great deal of light and very strong water flow, which may not be ideal for certain seahorse species.

Chapter 4: Buying your seahorse

1) Wild caught, tank raised or bred in captivity?

The general consensus is that seahorses bred in captivity offer advantages over ones that have been caught in the wild. In fact, most breeders and aquarists say, "only buy captive bred seahorses!" There are several reasons for this recommendation.

Firstly, buying specimens that have been bred for aquariums and tanks reduces the demand for wild-caught seahorses, which in turn protects wild seahorse populations.

Secondly, seahorses that have been raised in tank or captive conditions are used to having limited space and eating frozen and other food, which makes them much easier to feed and keep healthy. They therefore live far longer.

Finally, wild-caught seahorses often carry parasites and disease that they can deal with. However, if they and these organisms are introduced into a tank or aquarium, they can make all the other inhabitants sick.

The terms used in relation to seahorses, though, are more complicated than with most fish and can lead to some confusion:

Wild-caught

Wild caught is a fairly self-explanatory term: these seahorses were captured in the wild. As such, they present numerous disadvantages and risks.

Wild creatures that are captured, placed in a restricted environment and transported become highly stressed. As with all living creatures, stress impacts on the immune system and general health.

In addition, these fish usually have parasites – internal, external or both – and may also carry bacteria or viruses. This means they will have a shortened lifespan and they pose a significant risk to any other tank inhabitants.

They are also used to feeding in the wild and will rarely adapt to eating frozen or dried food. They may eat some live foods but often they stop eating and die.

Captive bred

As the name implies, these seahorses are born and raised in captivity. These fish are reared in sterilized seawater or artificial seawater and are accustomed to frozen and dried foods.

Some breeders use the phrase "true captive bred" to indicate that the parents and offspring that are for sale were born and raised in captivity.

Captive bred individuals are certainly the hardiest type of seahorse and the most likely, in the normal course of events, to live far longer than wild caught specimens.

Tank raised

One would expect "tank raised" and "captive bred" to be synonymous but they aren't. Literally, this of course means "raised in a tank". However, in practical terms there are other implications.

While captive bred seahorses are usually at least three generations away from the wild, tank raised seahorses are a very different proposition. In other words, their parents were living in the wild and the pregnant male was caught and gave birth in the tank. The young are then reared or raised in a tank.

From the perspective of a potential buyer, these seahorses are a better bet than wild caught but far from ideal as they pose many of the same dangers that wild caught do: parasites, bacteria, potential feeding problems and short lifespans. These seahorses are also often sold when they are too young, which causes them stress and can further compromise their health.

Variations of the standard terms

The terms "tank bred" and "captive raised" are the same as "tank raised", *not* "captive bred". Less scrupulous breeders use some of these terms to cause confusion and sell seahorses that are not ideal.

One should be careful to establish that a seahorse is "captive bred" before buying it. If a retailer is not sure of the origin of a seahorse, don't buy it!

2) Male and female seahorses

If one only wants to buy a single seahorse, the gender does not matter. Most aquarists strongly suggest that one obtains a pair. Solitary seahorses are usually lonely and sad creatures!

A bonded pair is of course preferable but not essential if you want to breed seahorses.

How one can tell of a fish is male or female

It is extremely hard, and sometimes completely impossible, to tell whether an immature seahorse is male or female. However, as they get older it becomes very easy: the male has a *brood pouch* and the female does not.

The brood pouch is found below the anal fin and it tapers down to the tail. When the male is pregnant, the pouch is no longer a gradual slope but bulges and protrudes very noticeably. The brood pouch gives the male a "D" shaped body.

The female's abdomen, on the other hand, joins her tail at a much sharper angle because of the absence of a brood pouch. She is more "P" shaped and the anal fin may be both higher and larger than the male's.

Other gender differences are:

- ✓ *Keel*: Males have a ridge, called the keel, running along the ventral side or front of the body. The keel is absent in female seahorses.

- ✓ *Snout:* The snout of the female is slightly longer. This is not a very reliable determining factor, as the difference can be very slight and therefore hard to spot in some species.

- ✓ *Tail*: Males usually have a longer tail in proportion to the trunk or body than the female does.

3) How to ensure the seahorse you want is healthy

While it is not possible to be 100% sure that a seahorse is free of disease and parasites, there are rules that should ideally be followed:

- ➢ Only buy *captive bred* seahorses.

- ➢ Only buy *seahorses that are eating* frozen food and a broad diet, as this usually indicates health and will make your life easier in terms of feeding.

- ➢ Only purchase seahorses from a *reputable dealer*. You can find the names of good dealers through aquarium or reef clubs. A good online retailer will offer a 5 to 7 day survival guarantee on fish that they ship.

Things to watch out for:

✓ The seahorse is active or at least looking around and alert
✓ It is eating well
✓ The rings are visible but not protruding too far, which indicates it is well fed
✓ The eyes are bright and are mobile and active
✓ The fins are clear
✓ The belly is slightly rounded.

What you do not want to see are any of the following:

❖ The seahorse is motionless and not interested in its surroundings
❖ It won't eat when offered food, including live food
❖ The rings are visible and the skin has caved in between the rings
❖ Its breathing is abnormal: panting, gasping, coughing (this causes the seahorse to jerk), gilling (breathing heavily) or frequent yawning
❖ The eyes are dull and motionless or protruding
❖ The skin looks flaky or very dry
❖ There are growths on the body or patches of inflammation that look red, grey, yellow or even white. Note, though, that some algae growth is normal.
❖ The gills look very red or inflamed
❖ The seahorse is lying on the bottom of the tank and / or not swimming normally
❖ Their faeces are white and string-like
❖ The tail is stiff or clearly painful because the seahorse is not hitching and won't balance on the tail tip
❖ The fins are discoloured or ragged
❖ The belly is very distended or bloated-looking.

If you observe any of these signs, don't buy the seahorse!

Chapter 5: What you need to buy for your seahorses

1) Essential basic equipment & supplies

While this is not necessarily an exhaustive list, it does give an indication of the basic items or supplies required in order to set up a tank or aquarium for a seahorse.

- Tank or aquarium of an appropriate size and height
- Hood or cover with strip light
- Water pump
- Substrate for the bottom of the tank or aquarium
- Décor (hitching posts, live rocks, coral etc.)
- Algae sheets or attack pad or a magnetic glass cleaner
- Filter with adjustable flow rate
- Thermometer
- Heater
- Full spectrum light
- Water conditioner
- Hydrometer or refractometer
- Aquarium salt
- Saltwater test kit
- Suitably sized net
- Siphoning hose
- Protein skimmer
- Appropriate food.

Investing in a book or two about marine aquariums generally and / or seahorses specifically (you may not find species specific books) is also strongly recommended. After these books have been purchased, they must be read with care; the more information you have the better... for your sake and the sake of the seahorses and all the other tank inhabitants.

2) The aquarium or tank

Seahorses require tanks that are large enough to contain the volume of water they need, long enough to allow for movement and deep enough to accommodate a fish that swims in a vertical position. Naturally, the larger the seahorse species, the bigger the tank must be.

Aquarists seem to agree that unless one is keeping the tiny Pygmy Seahorses, the minimum tank height (or depth) should be 74 centimetres or 29 inches.

A useful formula to use to calculate the minimum height is that a tank's height should be 3 times the uncurled length that the species of seahorse will grow to. Keep in mind that this must be the depth of *water*, not the depth of the tank, because the substrate will take up several inches / centimetres.

The minimum volume of water for a pair of seahorses is 20 gallons or 76 litres (US) or 91 litres (UK). For larger species the minimum is twice that or 40 gallons or 152 litres (US) or 182 litres (UK).

The tank must also provide enough space to accommodate the décor items they need such as live rocks or corals. Seahorses need horizontal space, so the tank should also not be too narrow.

Ironically, smaller tanks are far more work for the aquarist. The reason for this is that toxins build up much faster in a smaller tank or aquarium than they do in a large one. Toxins such as nitrates or ammonia have very negative effects on water quality.

This in turn has detrimental and potentially serious effects on the health of the seahorses and other species in the tank. It also leads to algae growth, which is both unhealthy and unsightly. A good filtration system is essential, but there is no substitute for regular water changes!

Chapter 6: Setting up the aquarium

Setting up an aquarium properly takes time and effort. However, this initial investment is well worth it, as it ensures a tank that is good to look at and – even more importantly – provides the right environment to keep your seahorses (and any other tank occupants) happy and healthy.

No step in the process should therefore be left out. There are, broadly speaking, 6 stages that one should go through:

1) Preparing the water for the aquarium or tank

This stage of the process involves several steps or aspects and they should be followed several days before any fish are introduced into the water:

- Install the water filtration system

- Treat the water you will use by reverse osmosis, if possible

- Add a liquid dechlorinator if you are using city water

- Add aquarium salt mix

- Check the salt / salinity / specific gravity levels using a hydrometer

- Adjust the salt levels as necessary

- Install and set a heater to the appropriate temperature

- Let the tank run for several days

- Monitor salinity and temperature regularly to ensure that the equipment is working as it should.

Some of these aspects, specifications and items of equipment will be discussed again in a later section of the book.

2) Building the aquarium or tank substrate

If stage 1 has run successfully one can then build the substrate or what is sometimes called the aquarium or tank's foundation.

Many specialists and retailers strongly recommend the use of an aragonite-based substrate, as aragonite is thought to be essential in replicating reef conditions. Not only is aragonite a material that sea life has evolved to live with and amongst and to use, it also keeps the tank or aquarium's pH level very close to its natural and correct one. An additional benefit of this natural mineral is that it has been scientifically proven to remove pollutants such as lead, zinc and cobalt from water.

In addition to substrate, one could add a layer (2 to 3 inches or 5 to 7.5 centimetres) of live sand. This type of sand contains microorganisms and bacteria that are beneficial to the tank or aquarium environment. One should ideally then add live rock that has been cured (the curing process will be described in the next section).

3) Curing live rock

Live rocks must be cured before they can be safely used. One reason that curing is necessary is that some of the organisms that lived on or in the rock die when the rock is removed from the ocean and transported. These microorganisms decompose and release ammonia, which is toxic. The curing process deals with this problem.

Some aquarists place the live rocks into the tank to cure and they change 25% of the water once a week. Others place the rock or rocks into suitable containers filled with water. In either event the curing process begins an essential nitrogen cycle, which ensures that any dead and decomposing organisms are removed.

Live rocks should be in water to cure for 4 to 5 weeks. They must also be kept in the dark during the curing process or algae will begin to form on them and this presents a whole new set of problems.

4) Placing live rocks

Live rock is an important décor item as it offers great benefits for the tank or aquarium. These rocks are aragonite-based and porous. What makes them "live" is the fact that microorganisms of various kinds, including 'good' bacteria, live in and on them.

The use of live rocks therefore offers a number of advantages. Firstly, the rocks add to the visual interest of the aquarium or tank and provide hiding places for some tank occupants. Secondly, the aragonite the rocks are made of help to maintain healthy water parameters. Furthermore, they provide nutrition to the creatures living in the tank.

There are several types of live rock that can be used in a tank or aquarium. These rocks vary in terms of shape, colour and the nature of the organisms on them depending on where they were harvested or which waters they are from. One needs to ensure that one selects rocks that are suitable for the seahorse species you have chosen. Live rocks are usually supplied with instructions, which should be followed.

When positioning the live rocks, one must leave an open path along the substrate. This allows seahorses to move across the substrate. Furthermore, with some species, the courting rituals involve the bonded pair moving or dancing across the bottom of the tank together.

If you only have seahorses in your tank you won't need many live rocks, as seahorses do not naturally live near rock walls and they are such poor swimmers that moving through tunnels in rock piles is just plain difficult. Seahorses are happiest with open spaces and hitching posts in the form of vegetation or appropriate branching corals.

When arranging the rocks, ensure that they are right side up. The side of the rock that shows the most colours should face upwards so that sponges and algae present on the rocks receive the amount of light they need.

5) *Lighting and items to combat algae in the tank*

Once you have cured the live rocks and run the tank or aquarium to make sure that the temperature and salinity levels are correct and constant, the next step is to test to establish that the levels of nitrite and ammonia in the water are as they should be: 0 parts per million! Once these elements are on track it is time to add the lighting.

Ideally, an aquarium or tank lighting system should be placed on a timer so that, even if you are not home, there will be light for the necessary number of hours each day. Seahorses don't actually require special lighting. However, other fish or the invertebrates in the tank or aquarium might. If this is the case, provide areas in the tank where your seahorses can get out of the light for a while. Exposure to light for 8 to 10 hours a day is optimal.

After light has been introduced to the tank, there will be a significant amount of algae growth or what is known as algae bloom. An aquarist wants to avoid this, as it impacts negatively on water quality, the health of the creatures in the aquarium, the way the tank looks, visibility and work load for you as you will have to clean the tank.

The way to avoid algae bloom is by using what is called an algae attack pack. These packs are a natural way of controlling algae growth and maintaining clear, good quality water. An algae attack pack does not contain chemicals, minerals or any artificial substances. Depending on the type of pack you buy you will be introducing any or all of the following into your marine aquarium:

- Hermit Crabs of various types
- Different kinds of marine snails
- Abalone.

Some of these or specific species of them are not compatible with certain seahorse species or seahorses in general. In addition, some can't legally be kept in some countries. This makes it essential that you check compatibility and legality before investing in one of these packs.

The algae attack pack is simply added to the aquarium just before the lights are put on for the first time. Each pack gives details of the acclimation or acclimatisation process required. The filtration system in your tank will then have to adjust to accommodate the new residents of your aquarium. The live rock or rocks will help with this process too.

When the algae pack snails and / or crabs have been in the tank for a few days you need to test the water again, focussing on nitrite and ammonia levels, as these will be affected by the new arrivals. Once the levels of these two toxins have reached 0, you can begin the exciting process of introducing your seahorses, other fish and invertebrates!

6) Introducing fish and invertebrates to the aquarium

As with other fish, seahorses should only be introduced to a tank that is mature. In other words, the tank has been set up and allowed to run until all the water and tank parameters are as they should be and are stable.

Before you can add your seahorses, it is helpful to go through this checklist:

- ✓ You have cured the live rocks you have used so they are not producing toxins

- ✓ You have arranged the rocks in such as way as to allow space for movement and free water flow

- ✓ The nitrite and ammonia levels in the tank are at zero and remain that way

- ✓ The temperature remains correct and constant

- ✓ The salinity levels are correct and constant

- ✓ The lighting and filtration systems are working correctly

- ✓ You have installed an algae attack pack that has acclimated

- ✓ There is no algae bloom

And, importantly:

✓ You have done research on the seahorse species and the various fish and invertebrate species you have chosen

✓ You have learnt all you can about general marine tank care

✓ You have made sure that the fish and invertebrates you want to place in your aquarium are compatible with your seahorse species!

If you can tick off each of these items you are ready to begin stocking your tank! However, there are a few rules that govern this exciting and fun stage of setting up a tank or aquarium:

● It is very important that you introduce stock gradually so that the various filtration systems – mechanical and biological – can adjust to each new batch of inhabitants.

● Begin with the shyest species because they need a chance to settle and establish themselves before the arrival of the more assertive species.

In terms of how many fish one can have in a tank or aquarium, there is a guideline rather than a hard and fast rule because it depends on several factors including the species involved and their requirements and temperaments.

7) Corals that are compatible with seahorses

One can use a number of corals and polyps in a tank or aquarium but not all of them are compatible and fairly easy to care for. The best options are generally considered to be:

- Mushroom, Hairy Mushroom and Toadstool Coral
- Leather Corals
- Sea Mat Polyps
- Green Star Polyps
- Yellow Polyps
- Moon Coral
- Pineapple Coral

- Raspberry Coral
- Clove Polyps
- Kenya Tree Coral
- Pulse Coral
- Ivory Coral
- Photosynthetic and Non-photosynthetic Gorgonians
- Pagoda Cup Coral
- Carnation Coral
- Disk Coral
- Orange Cup Coral
- Lobed and Open Brain Corals
- Pipe Organ Coral
- Caribbean and Indo-Pacific Ricordea
- Purple Sea Blade.

These various coral and polyp species are found in an astounding array of shapes, textures and sizes. Their colours range from muted greens to vibrant pinks, reds and blues. As a result, they add great visual appeal to an aquarium. They also perform important functions for the tank as a whole and for its occupants.

8) Waste management: a detritus attack pack

The final stage of tank or aquarium set-up is the addition of a detritus attack pack that contains those invertebrates that help to maintain the water parameters at healthy levels. An easier way to think of these creatures is as the clean-up crew!

The size of the pack you will need will be determined by the size of your tank. The snails and crabs that these packs contain are scavengers that help to keep the tank clean by eating leftover food, grazing on algae and even eating waste matter.

Be cautious when selecting members of the clean-up crew because some will eat seahorse fry or babies! Good choices are:

- ✓ Snails: Astraea, Turbo, Cerith, Nerite and Trochus

- ✓ Fanworms and Feather Dusters

- ✓ Fighting Conch

- ✓ Blue-legged Hermit Crabs

- ✓ Shrimps: Peppermint, Scarlet / Blood, Grass, Rock-pool and Skunk Cleaner

Without these creatures, waste matter will accumulate in the tank, encourage algae growth and have a very negative impact on the quality of the water and therefore the health of all the tank occupants.

Biological filtration systems like the marine creatures in the clean-up crew are especially important in a tank with seahorses because they are messy eaters and defecate frequently, as they have no stomach.

9) Air and water flow systems

The majority of the oxygen that is in tank or aquarium water is dissolved oxygen from the surface of the water. The water works the same way our bodies do, as oxygen is taken in and carbon dioxide and other toxic or unwanted gasses are released.

While the water surface does take care of much of the oxygen that the creatures in your tank will need, you will still need to get some kind of air system. There is a wide range of these devices available currently and you will need to select one based on the size of your aquarium or tank, the fish and so forth in it and your budget. It's a good idea to get advice from a reliable and honest dealer as it can become confusing.

The main types of air systems one can get are under-gravel bubble systems and air stones.

Both are driven by electrical air pumps. In terms of water flow or circulation, aquarists often use a combination of:

- Powerheads
- Wave-makers and oscillators.

Water flow rates

The flow rate is defined as the number of times in an hour that the entire volume of water in a tank moves through the pumps.

For many years it was thought that seahorses needed slow water flow or circulation rates. The root of this misconception might be the fact that these fish are such poor swimmers.

Consensus now seems to be that the flow rate should be between 10 and 20 times per hour. The way one can calculate is to multiply the volume of the tank by 10 to get the hourly rate of flow. For example, 20 gallons x 10 = 200 gph (gallons per hour) flow rate. You can achieve this by using, for instance, two 100-gph pumps or even four 50 gph pumps.

One should position pumps in such a way that there are places in the tank where the flow is less strong so seahorses can rest there if they need to. Intake pipes must not be too large and should be covered so seahorses are not sucked into or against pipes are killed or injured.

Under-gravel filters

As the name suggests, these fairly thin and flat filters are placed under the gravel or sand at the bottom of a tank or aquarium when you are setting it up. While they are actually there to aid with filtration and water quality, they also release air bubbles, which move the water up to the surface. This helps with the exchange of various gasses into and out of the water.

Other advantages of these filters are that the bubbles that are released are attractive and these items of equipment are relatively inexpensive.

On the down side, some tank owners find the constant sound made by the bubbles irritating. Others find it soothing…

Air stones

Air stones are very popular with a lot of aquarists. However, the bottom line is that they are *not* recommended for seahorses because they produce small air bubbles, which can cause or worsen air bubble disease in male seahorses.

Powerheads

A Powerhead is an electrical unit that can be safely submerged in water. This is thanks to the fact that they are sealed. They can be positioned on the bottom of a tank or attached to the sides. While Powerheads are used to run or power various pieces of equipment in an aquarium such as various types of filters, protein skimmers and air pumps, they are also ideal for water circulation. Naturally, the larger the tank, the more Powerheads one must use.

The basic advantages they offer an aquarist are that they are very effective, economical in terms of power consumption and they are fairly inexpensive. They make the tank a healthier environment for all the inhabitants because of the strength and consistency of the water flow they generate. The associated benefits include:

- Greatly improved water quality

- Improved oxygenation, which promotes the health of the tank's occupants

- Reduced detritus in the tank by improving filtration

- Algae growth is deterred or significantly reduced

- Food brought to stationary creatures in the tank

- The tank inhabitants are stimulated to move and so get exercise, which improves their health.

All of these are due to one factor: the steady and strong water circulation throughout the tank or aquarium generated by Powerheads.

While there is no doubt that buying a Powerhead is an excellent investment, it is also necessary to place them with care and caution. For instance, some anemones and corals thrive in a strong current, while others will not flourish at all.

Seahorses require moderate currents, specifically a turnover rate of 10-20 times the water volume in the tank per hour. This means the Powerhead must be placed where it will not adversely affect anything in the tank.

There is a wide range of Powerheads available on the market and this can be confusing. Here are some tips to guide you in terms of choosing a suitable and reliable Powerhead for your aquarium or tank:

- ✓ Spend a little more money to buy a brand name Powerhead such as one manufactured by Hagen or Marineland for example. If you do so you can rest assured that you are getting a reliable product that is tested and should last. 'Budget' versions may cost less initially but they are far more likely to burn out.

- ✓ You need to invest in a Powerhead that you can get parts for easily if you need them. It also helps if the unit can be opened and disassembled and then reassembled easily for repair purposes.

- ✓ The interior may need cleaning from time to time and this is another reason why it should be a unit that can be opened with ease. If you can't clean the interior regularly or as necessary, it may burn out if it becomes clogged.

✓ A good Powerhead will be moisture proof and, preferably, epoxy sealed. This will prevent both water getting in and electricity leaking out!

✓ Buy a model that has a screen of some kind that will prevent any of the seahorses, other fish or invertebrates in your tank accidentally being sucked into the intake hole of the Powerhead.

✓ Intakes should be covered for seahorses, particularly the smaller species and if there are fry in the tank. However, one must make sure the holes in the screen or cover are not too small because they will clog up with dirt very quickly. This in turn will reduce the water intake, which can lead to the motor becoming overheated or even burning out.

✓ The model you buy must also be saltwater safe if you are placing it in a marine or saltwater aquarium. Not all Powerheads are able to cope with saltwater.

✓ If possible, select a Powerhead that allows you to adjust the water rate. This will mean that you can reduce or increase the rate of flow (or even reverse it) depending on the needs of your tank and its inhabitants.

✓ As an optional extra, you could purchase a directional flow diffuser that fits onto the Powerhead. This will enable you to direct the water flow in your tank with even greater accuracy and care.

Once you have selected the model you want, you need to decide how many Powerheads you need and where you will place it or them in your tank. The size of your aquarium is the most significant factor.

If you have a tank that is 20 gallons (91 litres UK or 76 litres US) or less you have two options: a single large Powerhead or two less powerful ones that can be placed at either end of the tank. Medium to large tanks will need more units and more powerful ones. Often a smaller unit is placed at each corner.

The bottom line is that you need as many Powerheads as it will take to create the amount of water circulation or flow that your tank requires in order to maintain good water quality.

The final important aspect of Powerheads is flow rates. These will also depend on whether you have a tank that only contains fish or a reef tank as one would have with a seahorse. Most experienced hobbyists believe that the water in the tank should be turned over, or circulated throughout the tank, between 6 and 10 times an hour. A few aquarists say that reef tanks should have a flow of 15 to 20 times an hour.

What is essential is that a balance is struck between:

- Circulating the water so that it and the tank inhabitants get all the benefits

- Not making your seahorses or fish swim against currents constantly, as this will exhaust them, or creating such strong and constant currents that invertebrates are damaged or harmed.

Wave makers and Oscillators

Wave makers are connected to controlling devices that turn the Powerheads on and off at set and regular intervals. This creates a variable current and waves.

Oscillators, on the other hand, create random currents by rotating the Powerhead rather than turning it on and off.

10) Protein Skimmers

In this context "protein" refers to the muck that floats around in the water. It consists of bits of uneaten food and waste matter of various kinds. This must be removed from the water and doing so is achieved through skimming or, to use the correct technical term, the process of "foam fractionating".

This sounds complicated and impressive but it isn't. Skimming is quite simply using water bubbles to remove protein molecules from the water.

What happens is that as the column or columns of air bubbles rise from the floor of the tank or aquarium, the molecules of protein attach themselves to the surface of the bubbles. These waste products rise to the surface of the water, where they are collected in a container.

The trick to successful skimming is that there must be a large number of bubbles because the more bubbles there are, the more protein will be collected. In addition, the longer the bubble column, the better, as this gives the bubbles more time to attract protein molecules to them. Furthermore, the smaller the bubble, the more slowly it rises and the more effectively it gathers protein molecules. In summary, bubble columns should:

✓ Contain a lot of bubbles
✓ Be as long as possible
✓ Consist of small bubbles or at least some small bubbles.

There are two types of skimming apparatus:

▪ Co-current: These have a vertical column of bubbles. These bubbles follow their natural tendency to rise to the surface. When they reach the surface of the water they burst and leave the proteins behind, often in the form of foam. Skimmers like this that use vertical bubble columns are known as co-current skimmers.

▪ Counter-current: These skimmers force the bubbles downward through the water or even sideways. Again, this is in order to keep the bubbles in the water for as long as possible so that they collect the optimal amount of protein.

In either type, the air that is used to create the bubbles is usually sent into the skimmer by means of a diffuser such as an air stone or an air pump.

What to Look For in a Protein Skimmer

As with other pieces of tank equipment, there is a wide range of skimmers from which to choose. There are some things that you should look for in a protein skimmer or a foam fractionating system:

- Look for a skimmer that is easy to maintain. You don't want a model that is difficult to work with so that you battle to remove, for instance, the collection container.

- The skimmer should be adjustable so that you can change and manage the water flow in the skimmer's reaction chamber. A manufacturer's claim that "No adjustments are needed" often actually translates as "No adjustments are possible"!

- You need to know where you are going to put the skimmer in your tank or aquarium. That will help you decide which model to get as some are placed in the tank and others on it.

As with any aspect of tank or aquarium equipment, don't ever be reluctant or afraid to ask for information and advice!

11) Heating / Temperature control

Fish are not able to raise and lower their body temperature in response to the environment as we are. It is therefore the tank owner's responsibility to provide heat – and cooling at times – and to maintain the correct temperature for the creatures in the aquarium.

The required temperature or the temperature range depends on the species of seahorse you have in your tank. You therefore need to establish what the species-specific temperature range is. It is also essential that the temperature remains stable. Using a high quality heater will go a long way to ensure this.

There are two health-related reasons why temperature is so very important:

o Seahorses are highly susceptible to bacterial illnesses thanks to their primitive immune systems. Bacteria flourish and multiply much faster in warmer water, so if the temperature is too high your seahorses are far more likely to get sick.

o Warmer water is not as rich in oxygen and while this is not good for any fish it is especially so for seahorses because of their unique gill structure.

Types of heating units

As with all the other items for your tank, you will be faced with a choice when it comes to buying a heater for it. There are three options in terms of heating systems:

- *Heating cable systems*: These are placed under the substrate of the tank and are connected to an electronic controlling unit. While these systems are more often used for fresh water tanks, some marine or saltwater aquarists do use them.

  The primary advantage of cable heating systems is that they distribute heat very evenly throughout the tank. This is mainly due to the fact that heat rises.

  However, there is a major drawback with them, especially for those who have a reef tank for their seahorses. If the system goes wrong and must be repaired or replaced you will have to remove everything from the tank before you can remove it from under the substrate!

- *Submersible heaters*: These heaters can be mounted from the side of a tank or placed on the substrate. Because they are fully submerged in the water, they heat the water very effectively. They are also easy to lift out if necessary.

- *Hang-on-tank heaters*: These, as the name implies, hang on the interior of the tank. They are only partly submerged beneath the water line. While they, too, are easy to remove if needs be, they are not efficient heaters because they are not fully submerged.

Words of caution

One must make sure that the heater is covered by a guard so that a seahorse can't stick to it and get burnt!

If you opt for a submersible or hang-on heater it is a good idea to have one in reserve. This way if the heater malfunctions or breaks down you have a backup unit available. Sometimes one doesn't have time to get a new one before the temperature in the tank changes significantly...with lethal results.

If you have a medium or large aquarium you will need more than one heater anyway in order to maintain constant temperatures throughout the tank. In this situation you should also have a heating unit in reserve.

Regardless of which type of system you select, remember to make sure that it can be used in saltwater and is not only suitable for fresh water.

Other factors to consider

When selecting and installing a heating unit or units you need to keep in mind that it or they won't be the only source of heat. Some heat will be given off by lights, other tank equipment such as Powerheads, heating sources in the room such as vents or central heating units and even the seasonal temperature extremes in your area make a difference to the ambient temperature in the room.

All of these heat sources and temperature factors will affect the temperature in the tank. This, in turn, will impact on your decision about the size heater your aquarium will need.

Fortunately there is a rule of thumb used by aquarists that will be of help: allow approximately 4 watts per gallon of water. Once you have calculated how many watts your tank will need you can work out the size of the heater and the number you will need.

How to deal with an overheating crisis

The inhabitants of a tank or aquarium are very susceptible to changes in water temperature. Even a couple of degrees can pose a huge danger to seahorses! Water that becomes too warm is fatal even faster than water that has become too cool. Tank owners who battle the most with this are those in very hot climates. However, it can affect other aquarists too.

Regardless of the reason for it, an overheating problem must be resolved as fast as possible. There are things that can be done quickly and without special equipment:

- o *Open or remove covers or hoods*: A cover or hood on a tank or aquarium traps heat. If the cover on your tank is hinged, you need to open it and leave it open until the crisis has passed. If there is a lid on your aquarium, you need to remove it and leave it off for as long as necessary (consider not putting it back because using a hood or cover is not generally recommended because they reduce aeration, lower oxygen levels and increase carbon dioxide levels).

- o *Fans*: Place small fans near the tank or clip-on fans on the sides or top of the tank. The fans should be directed in such a way that the air flows across the top of the water. The flow of air should be strong but not so much so that it causes any significant surface disturbance.

  By using evaporative cooling one can reduce water temperature by 3 to 5 degrees. The problem with this method is that water is lost, so one must watch the water level and top it up if needs be.

- o *Air conditioning*: Reducing the temperature in the room the tank is in can help to cool the water. However, this is not a quick solution and air conditioning units can be costly, even smaller portable ones.

- o *Adjust the lighting in the tank*: As mentioned earlier, lights generate heat in addition to illumination. Different types of lighting give off varying amounts of heat. Fluorescent lights produce the least amount of heat and metal halides the most. An easy way to reduce heat, therefore, is to have 'hot' lights on for fewer hours each day or, alternatively, only have the fluorescents on. You could do this for up to 2 days without impacting negatively on the tank's inhabitants.

o *Reduce the equipment in the tank*: All equipment generates some degree of heat. If that equipment is submerged in the water, it is going to heat the water too. As a longer-term solution one could think about using a single, more powerful unit rather than multiple smaller ones. For example, one 300-gph pump rather than three 100-gph pumps.

o *Clean equipment:* Equipment like pumps produce more heat if they are not clean because there is more friction in the motor. Keeping pumps clean by soaking them in vinegar every few months will lower the amount of heat they produce.

o *Upgrade or replace equipment*: Aging equipment becomes less efficient and can generate more heat as a result. Replacing items that are simply not functioning optimally will improve water quality and reduce heat.

o *Place equipment outside the tank:* One can replace some items of submerged equipment with external versions. For example, a submerged pump can be replaced by a motor that is external or outside the tank.

o *Use ice*: This is also not a complex solution but it is both effective and quick in an emergency. It's a good idea to keep a few ice packs in the freezer in case they are needed…You need to begin by removing some of the water from your tank because the water level will rise when you introduce the ice.

You can use plastic bottles that you filled with water and frozen or sealed bags that contain ice cubes. Either type can be placed into the tank, where they will float. Don't use ice cubes, as they will dilute the water and may alter parameters such as salinity and pH.

A further danger is that this is a pretty extreme method, over which the aquarist has little control.

o *Buy or make a chiller*: You can buy a chiller from a retailer if you wish to do so, but be warned: they are expensive. More practical aquarists make their own chillers using ice, an ice chest, a water pump and plastic tubes. There are a number of plans and ideas for DIY chillers available on the Internet.

With any and all of these methods it is essential to monitor the temperature regularly. The last thing one wants is for the water to go from too warm to too cold! In order to monitor it accurately you will require an accurate thermometer of some kind.

12) Thermometers

Thermometers are no different in that the aquarist is spoiled for choice. You can get one that gives readings in either Fahrenheit or Celsius or both. While there are many kinds of thermometers, they all do the same job. This can make selecting one harder. What can be helpful is to look at the pros and cons of each type.

■ *Floating thermometers*: This is perhaps the most widely known and earliest kind. They are inexpensive, easy to read, compact, and can either be left to float around or be attached to the side by means of a plastic suction cup.

The downside is that the suction cups wear out and must be replaced regularly, or are not effective and don't adhere properly, but if the thermometer is free floating it can bang into the glass sides of the tank and break, as these thermometers are also made of glass. In addition, the numbering is small and can be hard to read. Finally, if it is floating, one has to look for it each time.

- *Magnetic thermometers*: These thermometers offer a great deal. They are easy to attach: the thermometer is positioned against the glass on the inside of the tank and the magnet is placed outside the tank. They are held firmly in place, have easy to read numbers, a broad temperature range and don't corrode.

  The only disadvantage is that the white plastic casing is not attractive and makes these thermometers highly visible.

- *Stainless steel thermometers*: These, too, are inexpensive types of thermometer and they are usually just mounted to the edge of the tank. Because they are made of stainless steel, they don't corrode or rust. They are easier to read than the smaller glass thermometers.

  However, because they are fairly large and shiny, they can look unattractive. They also sink if they are dropped or knocked off the aquarium rim.

- *Standing thermometers*: These are compact, affordable and easy to read. They are weighted so they sink to the bottom but remain vertical. However, they come with a host of drawbacks.

  They have a tendency to move around with the currents and can bang against hard surfaces such as rocks or the sides of the aquarium. This makes these thermometers susceptible to breakage. They can also be hard to spot because they move and hard to read as they may be behind or against something.

- *Stick-on Liquid Crystal Display (LCD) thermometers*: These are the easiest thermometer type to install as you just peel off the backing and stick it onto the outside of the tank. Other advantages are that they are low cost, available in a range of sizes and various temperature ranges.

  However, the lamination may separate over time and they can be difficult to read.

- *Remote Sensor Digital thermometers*: Hardly surprisingly, these thermometers are not as inexpensive as others, but they are still not too costly. The advantages include their compact size, the fact that they are easy to read and that the LED display is placed on the outside of the tank or near the tank. A sensor cord runs from the display into the water and this is part of why these thermometers also have disadvantages.

  The LCD is attached by means of suction cups, which are not always effective and will need replacing. The length of the sensor cord dictates where the LCD can be placed. In addition, the batteries that power the thermometer will need periodic replacing.

- *Submersible LCD digital thermometers*: This kind of thermometer has a great deal in their favour: they are compact, fixed in place, have an easy to read LCD display and they are wireless and fully submersible.

  They are attached by means of suction cups, which can be problematic and will need to be replaced, as will the batteries that power the thermometer. Not all of these types of LCD thermometer are suitable for saltwater aquariums, so one needs to check on that.

- *Temperature Alert Remote Sensor digital thermometers*: These thermometers cost a little more than most others but they are compact and easy to read thanks to the LED display. The biggest selling point is the fact that these thermometers include automatic temperature setting high/low alarms, which can be extremely useful, especially if you have seahorses.

  The length of the sensor cord will limit where the LCD can be placed and the cord is visible. The batteries will of course require periodic replacing. These thermometers are made in either Fahrenheit or Celsius so you need to check that before buying one.

If you feel confused or simply overwhelmed by the range of types of thermometer available, you can find more information and advice online or from a retailer who is familiar with aquariums and the equipment that is necessary for them.

13) UV Sterilisers

An Ultraviolet or UV Steriliser is used to stop free-floating microorganisms from spreading in a tank or aquarium. This in turn serves to control infections and cross-infections between fish, invertebrates and corals. It does so by using UV light to kill these free-floating microorganisms. They have no effect on microorganisms etc. that are already in or on marine creatures. What is essential is that the UV steriliser is installed and operated correctly!

These sterilisers work by exposing the water that flows through them to UV light from their bulbs. The wavelength of the light is about 254 nanometres or 2537 Angstroms and this irradiates the water as it passes through the steriliser. The effect on bacteria and algae is to mutate its DNA, which in turn prevents them from multiplying or growing.

These sterilisers, if properly used, are said to be effective against algae, bacteria, parasitic protozoa and viruses. The larger the organism, the higher the required dose of UV will be. For instance, algae must be exposed to far higher doses than a virus has to be.

A UV Steriliser will produce different amounts of light depending on the wattage of the bulb: the higher the wattage, the more UV light. It's important to remember, though, that these bulbs degrade with age and must be replaced every 6 months or so.

There are several factors that impact on the effectiveness of a UV Steriliser that should be kept in mind:

- UV light is far less effective at sterilizing water that is murky or dirty. The UV Steriliser must therefore be placed after the filters so that the water is as clear as it can be.

- The UV lamp must be kept clean, because if a film or layer of deposits of some sort covers it, it will not give off as much UV as possible.

- UV can only penetrate 5mm (a mere 13/64") into salt water. This means that the lamp must be very close to the water.

- Not surprisingly, the longer water is exposed to UV, the more microorganisms will be killed. The length of time the water is exposed is determined by the flow rate: the slower the flow, the longer the exposure. Using a long bulb will also increase the exposure period.

- Temperature is a further variable that plays a role, because UV is optimally produced in warmer temperatures (104 to 110° Fahrenheit or 40 to 43° Celsius). Using a sleeve around the bulb can help to insulate the bulb against the colder water in a saltwater or reef aquarium.

While a UV Steriliser certainly offers very significant benefits, they do have a downside:

- They are of no use against any of the disease-causing microorganisms that are not free swimming and against string algae.

- UV can also destroy beneficial bacteria that live in substances such as substrate.

- UV light can destroy the properties of some medications that are in the water. In order to prevent this "denaturing" of medication, the UV should be switched off until the treatment is completed.

- They can cause a rise in water temperature and a chiller may have to be used to counteract this.

It is also important to keep in mind that they don't replace filters and good water quality parameter controls. UV is a nice-to-have extra form of protection.

Chapter 7: Water & other parameters

1) Salinity and pH levels

Salinity

Salinity refers to the levels of dissolved salt in water. In a marine tank that is home to a seahorse, the salinity levels should range from 1.021 to 1.026 grams per kilogram or 0.036 to 0.0362 ounces.

As with the other water parameters, you need to check them for all the species in your tank so that they are happy and healthy.

Acidity / alkalinity (pH)

Maintaining the correct pH level is a very important part of caring for a tank and keeping fish healthy. Power of Hydrogen, or pH, is the measure that tells one if something is acidic or alkaline. A pH reading of 7 is the neutral border between the two. Readings below 7 indicate acidity and those above 7 are alkaline.

Acids can be caused by several things in a tank or aquarium, but most commonly by:

- Waste in the tank that is not effectively removed by filtration and protein skimming
- Too much carbon dioxide (CO_2) because of poor water circulation and gas exchanges and, finally, nitric acid released by biological filters such as live rocks.

Both of these build up in the water and drop the pH level dangerously if they are not dealt with.

The oceans and seas have a way of combating all of these acids: they contain what are called "buffers". These consist of various chemicals including hydroxide, calcium, carbonate, bicarbonate and borate. They slow down the drop in pH levels. In order to deal effectively with acidity in a tank, an aquarist must make use of the same buffers.

Ways to avoid pH problems in your tank

The best way to avoid pH problems is to do regular partial water changes - which restore the buffers - and to make sure that the tank stays free of the factors that release acids into the water.

One can also invest in a piece of equipment simply called a "doser". This item will automatically introduce a range of supplements and trace elements, including buffers, into the water.

Calcium reactors are also an option to deal with severe or frequent problems with pH levels. They are costly, though.

Ways to combat pH problems in your tank

If you already have a pH problem in your tank, you need to deal with it very fast and effectively or you run the risk of losing your tank's inhabitants. The most common options are:

- ✓ If the pH is too low you can add either a pH increaser that you can buy at a retailer or you can add bicarbonate of soda, also known as baking soda.

- ✓ If the pH is too high, home remedies to reduce it include adding small amounts of lemon juice or vinegar to the water. Alternatively, you could buy a commercial pH reduction product.

Many aquarists believe that the three most important aspects of tank health are water temperature, pH levels and water quality.

Although tanks that only house fish can have a wider pH range, reef tanks such as the ones seahorses require must have a constant pH level. The pH level must be between 8.0 and 8.4.

2) Phosphate and Calcium

Phosphate (PO4)

Phosphate (PO4) is a compound of Phosphorous (P), which is a trace element that is found naturally in seawater and is essential for marine and reef aquariums. In the ocean, the levels of PO4 is 0.07 parts per million (ppm).

The reason why phosphate levels are of such concern to aquarists is because these compounds are the main source of food or nutrition for various types of algae. So, if there are too many phosphates in a tank, there will be significant algae blooms.

Brown algae grow on coral and this has two effects. Firstly, the algae growth dulls and obscures the colours in the coral, causing it to go brown. The covering of algae also results in the coral being unable to absorb the calcium it needs to grow its skeleton.

Phosphates are caused by several factors but the most common ones are the use of unfiltered tap water in the tank either as top-up water or to make up sea salt mixes and substances put into the tank such as foods, activated carbon and even some salt mixes.

For this reason it is strongly suggested that you check ingredient lists on all products so that you make sure you are not introducing phosphates or other unwanted compounds or trace elements such as nitrates, for example.

In a reef tank or aquarium, the Phosphate range should be 0.05 to 0.1 ppm. Since a minute quantity such as this is very difficult to access, you will need to invest in a very reliable and accurate test kit. Various reputable websites recommend test kits manufacturer by LaMotte and Hach. However, your local retailer will be able to offer advice and suggestions.

What one does need to remember is that, while the range might look miniscule, it is vital not to let the levels of Phosphate in a tank get too high. There are several things you can do to prevent phosphate build-up and to correct the level if it does get too high.

The first preventative measure is routine tank maintenance. If you perform regular water changes with good quality water, you will go a long way to controlling unwanted trace elements and compounds such as phosphates and nitrates. Routine and frequent tests are also necessary, because one can't assume that these elements are controlled just by the water changes.

If the phosphate levels in your aquarium are too high you can:

✓ Use commercial and easily available products that are designed to remove phosphates from tanks and aquariums. There is a range of these products on the market.

No matter which product one uses, it is essential that they are changed and replenished regularly. If they aren't, they will become saturated with the compounds they have absorbed and will no longer work.

✓ Phosphate levels are also reduced if you add a limewater or *kalkwasser* (KW) solution to the water. Limewater is essentially a diluted form of calcium hydroxide, which is believed to effectively remove phosphate because it contains very high levels of calcium.

✓ The Vodka Method also removes phosphates (and nitrates) but only when used with a protein skimmer. As the name implies, one adds a small amount of Vodka, or ethanol, to the tank water.

Calcium (Ca)

Without calcium in the water in which they live, many molluscs, crustaceans and corals simply can't grow and survive. These life forms extract calcium from the water and use calcium carbonate to build their skeletal structures. There is a complication, though: even if there is calcium in the water, it can't be used if the pH is not as it should be.

If both calcium and alkalinity levels in the water are low, calcareous life forms such as those mentioned will not grow or thrive and will die. Calcium, carbonate and pH / alkalinity are interconnected in marine or salt water.

The ideal calcium level in a tank is considered to be about 0.014 ounces per 33.8 fluid ounces US or 35.2 fluid ounces UK or 400 milligrams per litre. This level is slightly higher than those found naturally in the oceans. In order to introduce the required calcium into the tank water, one needs to use limewater or *kalkwasser* (KW).

In addition to reducing phosphates, KW also replaces the calcium that is absorbed and used by the organisms in your aquarium. The amount of limewater you add to the aquarium water will depend on its size and capacity. It will also be affected by the number and type of marine creatures in the tank that require calcium. This means that you may have to make constant adjustments if you introduce new inhabitants or if corals are in a growth phase etc.

Preparing a limewater or KW solution is not difficult but it does require care and safety precautions. The dry powder that is used is caustic and so you don't want to inhale it or have it in contact with your skin. Packets of the dry powder *must* be kept somewhere secure where children and animals can't get to it!

The powder is mixed with distilled or purified water. To this one must add either calcium oxide (CaO) or calcium hydroxide (Ca(HO)2). Some experienced aquarists use calcium chloride instead, but this is more complex to prepare and involves additional steps and chemicals. The recipe for the *kalkwasser* for a tank is simple:

i.   Add between 1 teaspoon and 1 tablespoon (most tanks will require 1 rounded teaspoon) of calcium oxide or hydroxide to 1 gallon (3.75 US or 4.55 UK litres) of distilled or purified water. It is suggested that one only make up this quantity at a time.

ii. Mix the power and water carefully and expose it to air for as short a time as possible. If a significant amount of carbon dioxide is absorbed by the mixture, it results in the formation of calcium carbonate and the loss of calcium.

One knows if this has happened because a white residue forms and settles at the bottom of the container or bottle. Any calcium carbonate must be removed from the solution before it can be used.

iii.   Keep the container sealed, because each time it is opened carbon dioxide will enter it, form calcium carbonate and destroy useable carbon. This is the main reason why one should prepare small quantities of the solution at a time.

Once you have the KW solution, you need to add it to your tank. However, it can't just be poured it; it must be introduced in a slow and measured way. Here again there are several options.

The first is the use of a commercial or DIY measuring pump or an "auto-doser". These are slow drip devices much like those used in drips in hospitals. They dispense a controlled amount of solution into the water at set intervals.

The solution is then circulated throughout the tank by the currents generated by powerheads, oscillators and so forth. The simplest way to introduce the solution is to add it to top-up water and pour this slowly into the aquarium, again letting the current do the in-tank mixing for you.

The most expensive option is to buy and install a calcium reactor. These sophisticated pieces of equipment mix and release the solution for you. They also generate the ideal pH for the mixture and greatly reduce the amount of carbon dioxide that enters the solution, so there is no loss of calcium through calcium carbonate formation.

The next option is to purchase calcium supplements that can be introduced into the water. If you use these products, you will avoid the measuring, mixing and adding. The price you pay will be, well, the price you pay for these not so inexpensive products.

3) The Vodka treatment

This was very briefly mentioned earlier, but this cost-effective remedy to reduce both nitrate and phosphate levels in a tank or aquarium justifies closer inspection. Although there are some aquarists that are very sceptical, others believe that using Vodka is effective. More accurately, one uses alcohol or 95% ethanol rather than Vodka.

Why this method works seems to be due to the fact that alcohol contains inorganic carbon. This type of carbon boosts the growth of bacteria in the water. These bacteria work with the aquarist because they actually incorporate or 'feed' on the phosphates and nitrates in the tank. The bacteria in turn are eaten or absorbed by some tank residents, like many species of sponge, or they are removed when protein skimming occurs.

The Vodka treatment is usually administered each day for three days and involves very small quantities. For example, if you had a 50-gallon tank (189 litres US or 227 litres UK), you would add 5 drops of 80% alcohol per day. This translates to 0.25 millilitres or an insanely small 0.0168 fluid ounces!

Chapter 8: Introducing seahorses and other creatures into the tank

Acclimation

After one has bought a seahorse, other fish and invertebrates, one can't just put them into the tank no matter how carefully it has been set up and prepared. Why? All the marine creatures you acquire will have been in water that will have different pH and salinity levels and temperatures to the water in your aquarium.

Marine animals are *extremely* sensitive to these factors. It is essential that they get used to the changes and differences gradually. This is the purpose of the process called ***acclimation***.

There are a couple of methods one can use. Regardless of which method you opt for, the golden rule with acclimation is not to rush the process. Both methods begin with these steps:

A. Turn off the light or lights in the tank and dim the lights in the room where you will open the box or container the marine creatures are in. Harsh or bright light and sudden exposure to light is very traumatic and will cause stress.

B. Place the still-sealed bag in the water in your aquarium. After 15 to 20 minutes, the water inside the bag will have slowly adjusted to the temperature of the water in the tank. By keeping the bag sealed you ensure that the level of dissolved oxygen in the water in the bag stays high.

The float method

Once you have completed steps A and B above, and have elected to go with the float method, you need to:

1. Cut the bag open just below the metal clip that seals it. Roll the edge of the bag down about 1 inch or 2.5

centimetres so that you create an air pocket in the rolled up section. This air should be enough to keep the bag afloat.

2. Carefully and slowly add a ½ cup of water from your tank or aquarium to the water in the shipping bag. Continue to add a further ½ cup every 4 or 5 minutes until the shipping bag is full.

3. Remove the bag from the water and drain 50% of the water, being carefully to disturb the occupants of the bag as little as possible.

4. Float the bag in the aquarium again and repeat step 2 until the bag is full once more.

5. Use a suitable net to carefully catch the marine creature or creatures in the shipping bag and release it / them into the aquarium.

6. Remove the floating shipping bag from the tank and discard the water. It's important that you don't ever place the rest of the water into your tank or aquarium.

The drip method

The drip method is considered to be the preferable one for certain fish and invertebrates such as wrasses, corals, star fish and shrimp. In other words, more sensitive creatures should be acclimatised using this method rather than the float method. The drip method does, however, require additional equipment in the form of air tubing and a bucket or buckets.

The bucket you use must be one that is only used for tank water to prevent possible contamination by, for instance, household cleaning products. Fish should be placed in one bucket and invertebrates in a separate one during acclimation. In addition, the tank owner must be involved throughout the process because progress must be monitored constantly.

The drip method begins with steps A and B of the floating method does. These steps balance the water temperature inside the bag. Once you have achieved this, you need to:

1. Empty the contents of the bag into the bucket. Remember to do this as carefully as possible so as not to stress or injure the marine creatures in them. It's also essential not to expose invertebrates to the air, so make sure they stay submerged as you empty the bag.

2. At this stage, the plastic tubing or pipes come into play. You need to run a drip line from your aquarium or tank to the bucket or buckets. It's important to control the flow so that the tube or pipe releases water very slowly. You could buy a control valve or make one by tying a fairly loose knot in the tube or pipe. It's also a good idea to fasten the pipe or tube to something so that it stays securely in place.

3. It's not difficult to begin the siphoning process for the drip method. Suck on the end of the pipe or tube until water begins to flow through it from the tank or aquarium. You must then adjust the knot or valve so that the pipe releases only 2 to 4 drips per second.

4. When the amount or volume of water in the bucket has doubled, you need to carefully and slowly discard half of it. Reinsert the tube and double the water volume again.

5. Transfer the fish and / or invertebrates in the bucket(s) to the tank or aquarium. Again, one must be very careful not to expose invertebrates to the air or to touch corals on their fleshier parts.

    If necessary, invertebrates can be scooped out of the bucket in a specimen bag and then the bag should be submerged in the tank. Once the creatures are out of the bag, seal it underwater and remove it from the tank. Be careful not to release too much of the diluted water into the aquarium. The water in the bag and bucket(s) must be discarded.

Specific gravity during acclimation

Furthermore, marine invertebrates and plants are even more sensitive than fish to changes in specific gravity. Specific gravity, very simply put, provides information about the concentration of solutions such as, for instance, salt water. Invertebrates require a specific gravity of 1.023 to 1.025 or they may become severely traumatised and stressed. Specific gravity must therefore also be carefully monitored during the acclimation process.

In order to test specific gravity, one needs to use a suitable tool such as a hydrometer or refractometer. Both measure specific gravity by measuring salinity or salt levels in the water. There is quite a debate about which is better. However, the majority of aquarists seem to feel that the refractometer is far more reliable and easier to use.

Corals and acclimation

There are some species of coral that produce excess mucous or slime during the shipping process. Once the coral has been acclimated, one should hold the coral by the rock or base and shake it gently in the shipping bag before placing it in the tank. One shouldn't be concerned if corals remain closed for the first few days. Once they have adapted and settled, they will open.

Some tips and rules with acclimation

o   Don't rush the acclimation process; be patient.

o   Some fish and invertebrates can appear to have died either before you begin acclimation or during the process. Don't assume it is dead. Continue with acclimation and quite often a marine creature will revive.

o   Don't expose invertebrates to air or handle corals roughly.

o   Don't place an air-stone or introduce air through a pipe or tube into the shipping bag or bucket(s). Doing so increases the pH levels far too quickly and will expose your marine creatures to ammonia, which is lethal for them.

o Keep the aquarium lights off for at least 4 hours after you introduce new fish and / or invertebrates to the tank or aquarium, as this will help them to adjust more easily to their new environment.

And a final thought...

There is a further stage that should be included as part of introducing new stock into a tank or aquarium: the use of a quarantine tank. A quarantine tank, as the name implies, is a separate tank in which new arrivals are kept for two weeks or so before they are introduced into the main tank.

Captive bred seahorses should be kept in quarantine for about 2 weeks. Wild caught and tank raised specimens should remain in quarantine for 5 or 6 weeks.

Using a quarantine tank greatly reduces the chances that newly arrived fish or invertebrates will introduce parasites or diseases that will infect your existing stock. It also gives the tank owner a chance to monitor the newcomers and make sure they are healthy, adjusting and eating well. It's not as easy to assess these factors once they are in with all the other creatures in the main tank.

Chapter 9: Caring for your seahorse

1) Basic maintenance

It will be no surprise by now to be told that a saltwater or marine tank is a lot of work. The fact that so many avid aquarists and hobbyists all over the world perform all the tasks that are necessary is proof of how wonderful having a healthy, colourful tank stocked with seahorses and other fascinating marine creatures is!

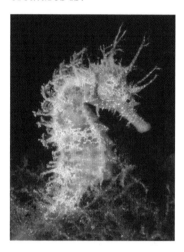

What can be very helpful is to draw up a schedule for regular and routine tank maintenance tasks. In addition to feeding the inhabitants of the aquarium, the owner needs to carry out of number of tasks regularly. The basic ones are:

o Clean out the filter
o Clean out the container connected to the skimmer
o Check the various water parameters: temperature, salinity, pH, calcium, phosphate and nitrates
o Check to ensure that all the equipment is still working
o Mix up solutions such as saltwater and limewater
o Replace 25% of the water in the tank
o Top up the tank
o Remove any dirt or detritus

o   Monitor the condition of all the seahorses, other fish and invertebrates in the tank.

These tasks are broken down by frequency in more detail later. As a rough guideline, it is recommended by experienced aquarists that one check:

-   Equipment: daily
-   Salinity: twice a week
-   Temperature: weekly

Water changes should be performed once or twice a month.

Tip: Unplug the heater or heaters before you work on a tank! If you don't, and water levels change in such a way that they impact on the heater and you run the risk of cracking or breaking the glass in the tank or overheating or even burning out the heater.

2) *Preparing water for your tank*

One can't – or certainly experienced aquarists very strongly advise against –using tap water in an aquarium because it contains substances that are damaging to the water quality and therefore to the creatures living in the tank.

If one needs to top-up a tank, replace some of the water or mix up a solution such as a sea salt mix, one must use treated tap water, bottled water, fresh sea water or distilled water that has not passed through copper pipes during the distillation process.

Why you shouldn't use tap water in an aquarium

The water supplied in towns and cities is put through purification processes. However, this does not mean it is safe to use in a tank. If one does use it, one is likely to encounter problems.

Tap water often contains chlorine and the attendant chloramine bonds. One can use a de-chlorinating product, but while they do remove chlorine, they don't usually break the chloramine bonds.

You could look for a product, however, that specifically deals with chloramines.

In addition, tap water contains metals and, sometimes, bacteria. There are often heavy metals such as iron and copper in this water. These are frequently lethal for the inhabitants of the tank. The bacteria may be there because some strains will survive the chlorine used to treat the water. Once these bugs are in your aquarium, they will have a chance to flourish and infect your precious marine stock.

Furthermore, tap water contains elements and compounds that do belong in water such as silicates, phosphates and nitrates. The problem arises because they often contain high levels or high concentrations of these substances.

As previously discussed, one already has to deal with some of these compounds when they are generated by marine creatures in the tank. Adding more causes headaches for the tank owner. The primary undesirable result of these unwanted compounds is various types of aggressive algae blooms in the aquarium.

Treating tap water

Treating or pre-treating tap water is not always a great deal of work but some options can be more expensive than others. There are various routes one can take.

You could treat tap water with chlorine in order to kill any bacteria that may be in it. This is a simple option but it is not a very good one for two reasons. Firstly, you will remove most or even all the bacteria but the water will still contain heavy metals like iron and copper, and minerals and trace elements such as nitrates and phosphate that will cause algae to flourish. Secondly, you will have to de-chlorinate the water before you can use it, because chlorine is also not a friend to your seahorses and the other marine creatures in your tank or aquarium!

As with so much else, you can choose the way you will obtain the clean, good quality water necessary for your tank:

✓ Use *a basic water filter*. This is the most cost effective option but not necessarily the best one in terms of quality. You can obtain a freestanding filter of some kind or one that fits onto the tap. The latter is less cumbersome and time consuming to use.

✓ A *carbon filtration system* is more effective than a regular water filter because these filters remove metals, phenols (acidic, organic compounds) and chlorine. A carbon filter is also said to reduce or even eliminate odours from the water.

There are various types of carbon and carbon-based filters that are commercially available, or one could make one.

✓ Perhaps the best type of water filter or filtration system is the *Reverse Osmosis (RO) or Deionization (DI) filtration unit*. The optimal system is thought to be one that is a RO DI combination.

These combined RO / DI systems are expensive but many aquarists believe they are worth the initial cost. The reason is that they save one a great deal by helping to preserve high water quality and so avoid many issues that are both difficult and costly to deal with. In effect, they are thought to pay for themselves.

✓ Instead of filtering water, you could *buy fresh, filtered water* from local water companies. It is very important, though, to make sure that the producer and bottler uses a good, reliable filtration system, preferably a RO / DI system of some kind.

✓ In order to avoid both filtering water and adding salt to it, you could *buy natural seawater* from a local aquarium, if you are fortunate enough to live near one, or from a company that sells salt water. The third option is to collect water direct from the ocean if you live at the coast and know the water to be good quality.

If you collect seawater yourself, you must choose a location with care so that you don't collect water that is contaminated. For example, don't take water from the ocean at a dock or harbour, near a river mouth, close to factories or farmlands or near manufacturing areas. All of these potentially leak or release toxins into the water.

✓ *Buy bottles of distilled water* from commercial companies. The only word of caution here is to ensure that the distiller does not use copper pipes, because if they do you may be introducing an undesirable metal into the tank water. You need to make enquiries about distillation processes before you use the water.

One factor to keep in mind when you are deciding on where and how you will get water is the size of the aquarium or tank. Naturally, the more water you need, the more expensive some options will become. Others will be ruled out simply because they are not feasible or practical for you.

Mixing salt water for your marine or reef tank

Preparing salt water for a tank or aquarium is not complex or difficult. However, getting the salinity levels and therefore the specific gravity right is essential for the health and survival of the marine creatures in the tank. There are a few things that must be kept in mind.

Firstly, one can't use ordinary or common table salt for a salt-water solution for a tank or aquarium. It's also not acceptable to use the various types of sea salt sold in supermarkets. Aquarists have to buy a good quality sea salt mix from a reputable retailer or online shop. There are various websites on the Internet that offer details of the mixes on offer and compare them so that you can choose the best one to meet your needs.

In order to prepare the sea salt mix, you need to use the correct kind of prepared water (as discussed earlier in this chapter). If you are starting out and setting up a new aquarium, you can mix the salt mix into the water in the tank. If you are topping up an existing tank, the solution must be mixed in a bucket or some other clean and suitable container before you add it to the tank water.

When you begin to add the sea salt mix to the water, you should begin with less of the mix than you anticipate needing. As with cooking, it is much easier to add more salt than take it out! The mix will also dissolve more quickly if the water is stirred. One should go on mixing until the water clears and no longer looks at all murky or opaque.

In order to assess the salinity or specific gravity levels in the water, you need to use a refractometer or hydrometer. One can't guess or make an estimate; it is essential that the ranges are correct.

Tips

If you are adding water to a tank that is running, you must also ensure that the water is at the right temperature and not only the correct salinity level. These levels must correct before the water is added to the tank.

Secondly, if you are pouring water into a tank, you need to do so very carefully so that the tank inhabitants are not disturbed or stressed and so that the tank's substrate is not disturbed.

Finally, once you have completed the process, you should rinse all of the containers and other items you used in fresh water before you put them away so they are ready for use the next time.

3) Topping up the water level in your aquarium

A lower water level in a tank or aquarium is largely due to fresh water evaporation. This would logically indicate that fresh water should be used to top up the tank.

However, it is vital that one check the salinity levels, as salt may have also been lost due to other factors such as "salt creep". If the salinity or specific gravity is too low, then topping up will need to be with salt water rather than fresh.

4) Dealing with "salt creep"

Salt creep takes place when salt water from a salt or marine tank splashes onto surfaces and items above the water line or even outside the aquarium. Once the water has dried or evaporated, salt crystals are left behind. It is these crystals that cause problems.

The first possible effect of salt creep is that water salinity decreases and unless levels are monitored regularly this can negatively affect the health and well being of the tank's inhabitants. Fortunately, testing specific gravity and adjusting salinity is not too difficult.

These deposits of salt can have serious consequences in and around an aquarium because salt or sodium chloride is a highly corrosive substance. The extent of the damage depends on the nature of material the salt comes into contact with and how long the exposure lasts for:

- Metal items rust and corrode, releasing toxic compounds

- Electrical items also become corroded and this can cause shorts or burn-outs and loss of power

- Light bulbs that are not in protective housing become encrusted and this reduces the amount of light they give off

- Sheets of plastic, acrylic and glass suffer from an effect called etching. White spots, lines or patches develop on the surface and cause them to become slightly opaque

- Surfaces and items around the aquarium such as carpeting, curtains and wooden surfaces can all be adversely affected as they become mildewed, mouldy or rotten from the damp and corrosive salt. Paintwork may even peel.

The good news is that one can minimise the damage done by salt creep in and around a tank. The golden rule is to remove the salt as quickly as possible; the longer it is in contact with a surface, the greater the damage will be. If one deals with salt water splash as part of daily tank maintenance, a great deal of damage caused by salt creep can be avoided.

Steps that help to deal with and counteract the damaging effects of salt creep include:

- ✓ Wipe down the sides of the tank, its stand, light fixtures and the hood or lid with a clean cotton cloth that you have rinsed in fresh water. This should be done regularly.

- ✓ A very small amount of white vinegar on a damp cloth can also be used to reduce etching. However, vinegar can be used on *external tank surfaces only*.

- ✓ Remove pieces of equipment that can be moved and rinse them off in fresh water.

- ✓ As part of maintenance, one should wipe down electrical outlet points, plugs and cords using a damp cotton cloth. These should only be wiped down when they have been unplugged.

- ✓ Keep the water level in the aquarium at or even slightly higher than the tank's trim line. Doing so should reduce etching along the water line.

- ✓ Place splashboards made of plastic or acrylic or even tiles on the walls close to the aquarium.

- ✓ Whenever possible, place electrical items at a distance from the aquarium where they are unlikely to get splashed.

- ✓ Position a plastic mat under the tank to protect carpets and flooring.

Some salt creep is inevitable in elements of a marine or salt-water tank but at least one can slow it down. By implementing the steps listed above, one can reduce the effects and even prevent unnecessary damage due to salt creep.

5) *Standard tank maintenance schedules*

Different tank owners will approach tank maintenance differently. The size of the tank and how many seahorses, other fish and invertebrates live in it also affects how often certain tasks must be carried out.

While there may be some differing opinions in terms of when to do what, all aquarists agree that regular, routine maintenance is essential. It can be helpful to break tasks down as follows:

Daily maintenance checklist

- Check and adjust the water temperature

- Check and adjust salinity

- Remove salt creep

- Ensure all the equipment is running correctly

- Remove uneaten food and other matter that will decay

- Observe all the inhabitants for signs of ill health and stress

- Empty and rinse out the protein skimmer cup

- Check for leaks

- Ensure that all cords and tubes are still correctly connected and not leaking.

Weekly maintenance checklist

- Test levels of nitrate, ammonia, calcium, phosphate and nitrite and take corrective steps if necessary.

- Test pH levels.

- If you have a lot of marine creatures in your tank, you must replace 10% of the water.

- Rinse out pre-filters, filters and the tube running to the protein skimmer.

- Remove any algae from the inside of the tank's sides by scraping it off or by using an algae magnet. These devices can be purchased from reputable retailers.

Bi-weekly to monthly maintenance checklist

One or two days before you do any major maintenance work on a tank, you must check the pH levels, as they do tend to drop over time. If adjustments are necessary, they should be made before you carry out any cleaning, as it will help to guard against pH shock.

Bi-weekly and monthly tasks are:

- Change 10% of the water in the tank or aquarium. A partial water change should in fact be done weekly if you have a lot of marine creatures in the tank.

- Remove algae, deposits and build-up on tank surfaces.

- Remove salt and calcium deposits from the light fixtures. Water in the form of a damp, clean cloth will work to remove salt.

  A small quantity of white vinegar on a clean sponge is effective against calcium build-up.

- Carefully vacuum the substrate to remove any debris.

- Check all equipment such as power sources for salt creep and related damage.

- Check the filters and replace disposable filters that have become dirty, clogged or saturated.

- Clear out the protein skimmer hose and valve. These valves and tubes can also be soaked in vinegar water to remove any calcium. However, they must be very thoroughly rinsed in fresh water afterwards.

Bi-monthly maintenance checklist

As with bi-weekly and monthly maintenance, one must test and correct pH levels a day or two before working on the aquarium.

- Clean out all tubes, hoses and pipes. Over time they become clogged by a build-up of compounds and detritus in the tank. An aquarium brush can be used to achieve this. Various sizes and thicknesses of brushes are available commercially.

- Avid and experienced aquarists also clean out important items of equipment such as heaters, powerheads and pumps.

- Remove any algae growing on submerged tank equipment. This, too, can be achieved by soaking the items in white vinegar, scrubbing them with aquarium brushes and then rinsing them thoroughly in fresh water.

- If your tank system uses activated charcoal for filtration, the carbon must be replaced. If it is left for too long the carbon becomes so saturated that it begins to release toxins and impurities back into the water.

Bi-annual and annual maintenance checklist

- Replace light bulbs or lighting tubes, because over time the colour and intensity of the light they provide changes either due to aging in the unit itself or damage from salt creep or calcium build-up.

6) Being prepared for power failures or outages

A loss of power is a fact of life for most people, as weather and the state of power grids can impact on the reliability of the power supply. Not having power can constitute anything from an inconvenience to a life-threatening situation.

For the creatures in your tank or aquarium the loss of power is always life threatening. Vital systems for aquarium residents are oxygen and temperature control. Filtration becomes a problem later than these two factors, but it too will become crucial. Light is more important for certain invertebrates such as corals than it is for seahorses. Tank owners must therefore be prepared for a loss of power.

The first option is *battery-operated systems*. There is a range of commercially available equipment that runs on batteries. These can provide oxygen, heat and filtration, all of which the fish and invertebrates in a tank require in order to survive. These systems are usually the least costly and even the easiest to put in place.

The second possibility is an *Uninterrupted Power Supply* (UPS) unit. These units are traditionally used to keep personal computers going for a while following a loss of power. However, one can also connect essential tank equipment to one. The benefits of a UPS unit are, firstly, that it will come on automatically and, secondly, more powerful units can run for longer than battery-operated equipment. The fact that the unit will come on automatically means that your tank's creatures will have emergency help even if you are not at home when the power goes out.

Finally, tank owners could invest in a *power generator*. Given they are not inexpensive to buy, they should be viewed as an investment that will prevent costly livestock losses. As an added advantage, if a larger and more powerful generator were purchased it would have the capacity to meet household power needs in addition to keeping all the aquarium systems running.

Generators are sold in several sizes or capacities and can run on diesel, petrol or even propane. Retailers and suppliers will be able to offer information and advice in terms of the best model and type for your specific requirements.

Regardless of which source of alternative and emergency power you select it will make a great difference in terms of ensuring your tank's inhabitants stay fit and healthy and reduce your stress levels in the event of a loss of power.

7) A summary of tank conditions

There's a great deal to remember in terms of the parameters for various water and other environmental factors in an aquarium. If various levels and conditions are not correct, a tank owner will be faced with high mortality rates amongst aquarium inhabitants, extra costs and a great deal of extra work.

A summary of the primary levels and parameters for the type of reef tank used for seahorse are as follows:

- Salinity / Specific Gravity: 1.021 – 1.026

- Temperature: Species specific!

- pH: 8.0 – 8.4

- Calcium: 350 – 450 parts per million (ppm)

- Nitrate: Less than 1.0 parts per million (ppm)

- Phosphate: Less than 0.2 parts per million (ppm)

- Magnesium: 1 250 – 1 350 parts per million (ppm)

- Iodine: 0.06 – 0.10 parts per million (ppm)

- Strontium: 8 – 14 parts per million (ppm)

- Ammonia: Should not be detectable

- Nitrite: Should not be detectable

Chapter 10: Feeding your seahorse

1) What to feed your seahorse

Seahorses are opportunistic predators that have voracious appetites. They ambush their prey and eat live, moving food. The reason they are described as opportunistic is they don't hunt but wait until food is close enough to be sucked up through their snouts.

They also have very short digestive tracts and don't have stomachs. This is the reason why these fish eat almost constantly in the wild and why they can't build up reserves in their bodies.

These fish do not have teeth, so prey is swallowed whole. The seahorse's diet consists of anything that is small enough to be sucked in and swallowed. The majority of food items consist of small crustaceans (amphipods, Mysis shrimp and crustacean's larvae), invertebrates and the fry of other fish. They do not, as some other fish do, eat dead or decaying matter. Baby seahorses eat copepods, which are tiny crustaceans the size of a full stop.

A good, varied diet for seahorses would consist of shrimp such as brine, red or ghost shrimp, frozen Mysis, krill, spirulina flakes and an appropriate dried, flaked food that can be purchased from a marine retailer.

2) How often to feed a seahorse

Seahorses need to be fed once or even twice a day. Some aquarists even feed their seahorses three times a day. As mentioned, in the wild these fish 'graze' all day, so having limited feeding times is not natural for them.

Certain factors, however, affect feeding frequency:

- The size of seahorse species you have
- How much food you dispense at a time

- How many other marine creatures there are in the tank
- The feeding routine that works best for you and your fish and invertebrates.

A point on which all aquarium owners do agree is that frozen foods must be thawed or defrosted before they are given to fish.

3) How much food to give your seahorses

It appears that, on average, a pair of seahorses can eat 3.5 ounces or 99 grams of food such as Mysis per feeding session. Keep in mind that it's not as simple as that if you have other fish in the tank. If the others are getting to the food first, your seahorses may not be getting enough to eat.

4) Dealing with excess food or leftovers

Uneaten food that remains in the tank and floats around in the water and / or gets stuck in cracks and crevices pose a health risk in the tank. This type of debris is dangerous because it can lead to algae blooms, bacterial outbreaks and reduction in overall water quality. With seahorses, there is an added danger because of their natural tendency to graze.

If there is too much leftover food in the tank it eventually settles on the bottom of the tank, where it will become home to bacteria and parasitic organisms. If a seahorse gets hungry it may eat some of these contaminated leftovers and could become very ill as a result.

A detritus pack or clean-up crew in the form of starfish, crabs such as hermit crabs and various types of marine snails help a great deal with this issue.

5) Tips and warnings about frozen food

The process of freezing can cause some nutrition to be lost. However, it's more complicated than that!

Seahorses benefit from, and enjoy, a diet that includes or consists of Mysis shrimp. This is bought in frozen form. If one doesn't know what to look for, one can feed seahorses Mysis that has almost no nutritional value or is beginning to spoil. In either event, it poses health risks to the seahorse.

Poor freezing and storage cause proteins to break down and vitamins are lost. In fact, each time Mysis is frozen there is a further breakdown of proteins. Furthermore, Mysis is high in lipids and fats, which are very important in a seahorse's diet. Unfortunately, these fats become rancid if the Mysis is not frozen and stored correctly.

Here are some hints and tips for selecting and storing frozen Mysis for your seahorses:

➢ The temperature that frozen Mysis should be kept at is -30° Celsius or -22° Fahrenheit. Regular refrigerators do not get this cold but commercial ones do.

➢ At the correct temperature, frozen Mysis can safely be kept for anything between 3 to 6 months but only if the cold chain has not been broken. If the Mysis is frozen, defrosted or partially defrosted and then refrozen, this period is dramatically reduced.

➢ It's better not to trust expiration dates and use Mysis long before them.

➢ Selecting a good batch of frozen Mysis can be a challenge. These selection criteria are helpful:

- Colour: The whiter the Mysis is the better.
- Packs: If there are visible air bubbles in cubes of Mysis, if flat packs aren't flat or if there are creases or crushed-looking sections or corners, don't buy it, as it has in all likelihood been refrozen!
- Packaging: If Mysis ordered online arrives partially thawed or not packed in gen packs or dry ice, send it back and don't use it!

Chapter 11: Health management

Setting up a reef or salt-water tank for your seahorse is a time-consuming and costly business. Once it has been done and you are carrying out routine maintenance, the last thing you want is an outbreak of disease in your aquarium.

Apart from selecting stock with care and monitoring your marine creature's health, there is another step you should take: make use of a quarantine tank.

1) A quarantine tank

What is a quarantine tank for?

Most aquarists or tank owners don't have a quarantine tank because of the expense of setting one up and the maintenance. However, quarantine tanks don't need to be big or costly. Furthermore, the benefits these tanks provide mean that they pay for themselves.

Quarantine tanks, as the name implies, keep new or sick fish or other marine creatures away from the others in order to prevent the spread of infections, parasites or other medical problems.

However, these tanks have a second, very important function and that is that they make it easier to treat or medicate sick fish. This second function of these tanks gives rise to their alternative names of treatment or hospital tanks.

When you are dealing with an infected seahorse or other kind of fish you need to do two things. Firstly, the individual or individuals must be kept away from the healthy ones. Secondly, you need to be able to medicate the sick fish without exposing healthy fish to medications that could harm them. Some fish medications can be particularly harmful to invertebrates.

By using a quarantine tank you can achieve both of these objectives and deal with the medical problem faster and without knock-on effects in the tank and on the tank's general population.

When a quarantine tank should be used

These important tanks are used on two different occasions. The first time a quarantine tank is important or useful is when you buy new stock for your tank. A quarantine tank allows you to isolate fish and invertebrates before you introduce them into the main aquarium. This gives you the opportunity to make sure that the newcomers are healthy. The second situation is when you discover a new fish or invertebrate or one in the main tank is sick.

Further benefits of quarantine tanks

There is a range of additional benefits associated with these tanks. Firstly, because quarantine tanks are usually fairly small (often about 10 gallons or 45.5 UK litres or 38 US litres or slightly more), one uses less medication and can monitor and control dosing far more easily. This also greatly reduces the risk of accidental overdosing. All these factors make treatment more effective and save you some money by not wasting medication.

In addition, it is much easier to watch and examine a sick seahorse in a smaller and less populated tank. One can assess physical factors such as movement, eyes, body and fin condition, breathing, growths and so forth.

With both sick and newly arrived marine creatures, a quarantine tank offers an ideal opportunity to make sure they are eating well and even what foods they respond to better. Again this is much harder or even impossible to do in a large or main tank.

Finally, a quarantine tank acts as a halfway house for newcomers where they can start to settle and recover from the stress of transport or shipping before moving into the main tank. This often makes acclimation to the main tank easier.

Setting up a quarantine tank

The equipment required for a quarantine tank is essentially a much reduced or streamlined version of what is needed for the large or main tank. In addition to the tank itself, one needs to buy a filter, a thermometer, an air pump, a heater and suitable lighting. Substrate is optional and décor other than a hitching post for seahorses is not required.

One must also have a dedicated water test kit and aquarium nets for use in the quarantine tank, as one can't use any equipment from it in the main tank or vice versa as this creates the risk of contaminating the main tank and its inhabitants.

It's a good idea to have a quarantine tank that is bare because porous materials such as rocks, sand and gravel can absorb medications. This means that your fish are not receiving the correct dose. Hitching posts should also be made of non-porous materials.

Deworming seahorses

When you place seahorses in a quarantine tank you also have an opportunity to deworm them. This is not a quick process but it can save a seahorse's life.

Deworming takes 9 weeks and consists of a program of feeding the seahorses food that has been gut-loaded with deworming medications and, at in the final stage, adding medicinal solution to the tank water.

This process is not 100% successful. An alternative is to observe the seahorse carefully for any signs of internal parasites. These include weight loss, known as wasting, or erosion of flesh.

The freshwater dip

A freshwater dip is recommended for captive bred seahorses but considered to be essential for wild caught and tank raised fish. The purpose is the removal of external parasites.

The water in the tank or container used for the dip must be the same temperature and pH as the quarantine and main tank. The difference is that the water is fresh and not salt. The seahorse should be placed in the dip for 8 to 10 minutes only and it must be observed throughout the process.

If the seahorse thrashes around or moves in a jerky fashion it usually indicates that it has parasites that are being killed by the freshwater. In other words, these movements indicate that the dip is effective. However, if the seahorse stops breathing for a marked length of time you need to gently and quickly remove it.

Why quarantine corals?

As with seahorses, there are two primary reasons to place new corals in a quarantine tank.

As they do for fish, these tanks offer corals a place to recover from the stress of being transported, settle and get used to their new environment. In this way-station tank the corals have an opportunity to acclimate to the new water and lighting.

Corals are prone to a host of parasites that you don't want in your main tank. If you place new corals in a dedicated quarantine tank when you first get them you will be able to examine them for presence of Limpets, undesirable Red Bugs and snail species, Flatworms and Nudibranchs.

One knows that corals are free of pests and parasites if, after a period in quarantine, they open or expand as they should and are colourful.

Quarantine tank maintenance

Ideally one should have one quarantine tank for fish and another for corals. It's also extremely important that the quarantine tank and equipment is disinfected between uses.

A mild (2-5%) chlorine bleach solution is an effective disinfectant for this purpose. However, one must ensure that all the chlorine is removed before using the tank again.

The quarantine tank and all the associated equipment must also be thoroughly dried because drying kills many aquatic pathogens but certainly not all of them.

2) Common seahorse illnesses and health problems

Common signs of illness in seahorses

Seahorses manage to resist illness and infection and play host to some parasites without compromising their overall health. However, that happy state of affairs only exists in the wild! In captivity it is unfortunately entirely different.

While one can acquire the knowledge to make a much more accurate diagnosis in terms of the health issue a seahorse is suffering from, there are some general signs and symptoms all tank owners should be on the look-out for:

- Loss of, or marked reduction in, appetite
- Weight loss characterised by highly visible rings
- Distended abdomen (except in pregnant seahorses, when it is normal)
- Listlessness: inactive and not looking around
- Breathing difficulty: gasping, gulping, coughing or yawning
- Unusual or erratic movements
- White spots or fungus on the body (some algae is normal)
- White, stringy faeces
- Inability to remain vertical
- Buoyancy problems (sinking to the bottom or floating)
- Clamped fins
- Unwillingness or inability to grip with the tail.

If you run the usual water quality and parameter tests and they are all as they should be, then you need to establish what specifically the seahorse is suffering from. If you don't feel up to the task, a vet or marine specialist should be consulted.

Preventing common health problems

There are steps that one can and should take that go a very long way to guarding against the common health issues that seahorses are susceptible to:

- ✓ Use a quarantine tank to screen new seahorses and isolate and treat sick individuals

- ✓ Maintain good water quality through testing, dosing when needed, regular partial water changes and maintaining the correct pH and salinity levels

- ✓ Ensure effective filtration, correct water temperature and lighting levels and adequate oxygenation

- ✓ Don't put too many marine creatures in an aquarium or tank, as overcrowding causes stress-related problems and cross infection

- ✓ Perform all the necessary maintenance on the tank to ensure optimal conditions at all times

- ✓ Use appropriate foods and feeding routines.

Seahorse diseases and ailments

A) Snout Rot

This nasty condition is caused by either a bacterial or a fungal infection. If it is bacterial, the snout is usually pinkish. If it is fungal, the discolouration is white. It is often triggered by poor water quality or stress.

Symptoms

The symptoms are easy to spot and fairly dramatic. The snout becomes both discoloured and swollen. In severe or advanced causes tissue on the snout is eroded and lost and other mouthparts become infected.

The condition also means that the seahorse initially loses its appetite and then, if the condition is left untreated, is unable to eat. Death is inevitable at this stage.

Treatment

Seahorses suffering from Snout Rot must be treated as early as possible and in a quarantine tank. They should be dosed with a medication that is broad spectrum and is effective against fungus and gram positive and gram negative bacteria.

Usually only a single dose is required, but in severe cases the ill seahorse may need a second dose.

B) Pouch Emphysema

The causes of Pouch Emphysema, more commonly known as Internal Bubble Disease, are not really known. What is certain is that only males are affected, as female seahorses do not have pouches.

Symptoms

These are easy to spot: the seahorse looks severely bloated and the pouch is greatly distended and is unable to swim or remain upright. Affected seahorses often float in a horizontal position.

As a result, the seahorse becomes stressed and is unable to feed properly. Secondary bacterial infections often set in and the seahorse won't eat.

Treatment

The only effective treatment for this condition is to remove the gas from the pouch as soon as possible. The first method is to massage the gas out. The second is more invasive and involves opening the pouch.

The male needs to be held underwater throughout the procedure. Hold him gently across the palm of your hand with his neck and head between the middle and index finger. Let him curl his tail around your little finger, as this will help to keep him in position. Don't squeeze him and wait until he starts to relax a little.

Use the index finger of your other hard to press gently from the tail or base of the pouch in an upward direction towards the pouch opening. One needs to gently ease the bubbles out of the pouch. Don't rub too hard or the seahorse's skin will be damaged and the movement must always be from the bottom to the top. One can also gently squeeze the sides of the pouch. If the process is effective, the bubbles will be visible as they emerge from the pouch opening.

If this doesn't work, one needs to use a blunt or smooth-edged implement like a pipette or soft plastic tube. Find the opening of the pouch (and this can take a while so it requires great gentleness and patience) and then ease the implement into the opening just enough to open it. The implement should not be pushed into the pouch, as this can cause internal injuries. One just wants to gently hold the pouch open to allow the bubbles to escape.

With either course of treatment it may have to be done more than once until the seahorse looks fine and behaves normally again.

C) Internal Gas Bubble Disease

As with pouch emphysema, the causes of this potentially fatal condition are not known. Likely theories are bacterial infection or even gas super-saturation.

Symptoms

The symptoms are bulging eyes (exophthalmia), visible external gas bubbles, severe bloating of the whole body, problems with buoyancy and difficulty moving. Affected seahorses also stop eating.

The main danger with this condition is that in severe or untreated cases the air places such pressure on the internal organs that they begin to fail. Some seahorses will starve to death before this stage is reached, however.

Treatment

There are two options here and neither is easy or guaranteed.

The first option is decompression. The sick seahorse must be placed in a tank that is a minimum of three times the depth of his or her normal habitat. The seahorse must be kept at the bottom of the tank for a minimum of three hours. Many hobbyists don't have access to a tank this large. Very sick seahorses will also not survive the treatment, as the organs are already too weakened.

The second option is less dramatic and has a higher chance of success: dose the seahorse with Diamox or acetazolamide. The dose is $1/8^{th}$ of a 250 mg tablet that has been dissolved in a cup of water. The medicine solution is injected into shrimp and two a day should be fed to the affected seahorses for a period of 4 days. This will only work in the earlier stages of the disease when the seahorse is still eating!

D) Flesh-Erosion Disease

This disease is caused by a severe bacterial infection. The bacteria involved are usually from the genus *Vibrio*. These infestations are usually the result of poor water quality.

Symptoms

The most obvious symptom of this infection is the damage to the flesh or tissue of the seahorse. The tissue becomes eroded and the site of infection becomes swollen.

As the infection progresses, the seahorse stops eating, the eyes become opaque or cloudy and the seahorse experiences severe breathing problems: they tend to breathe rapidly and appear to gasp and pant. Just the loss of appetite can lead to death in seahorses that need to eat a great deal.

In severe cases, the flesh is eaten away down to the bone. This awful condition leads to a painful death.

Treatment

Affected seahorses must be quarantined and dosed with strong antibacterial preparations. The medication must act on both gram negative and gram positive bacteria. Drugs from the tetracycline group are often the most effective.

E) External Gas Bubble Disease

The cause of this condition may also be bacterial or it might be gas super-saturation. Poor water quality or incorrect placement of some equipment such as powerheads may contribute to causing this condition, in which bubbles of gas form and appear just under the seahorses' skin.

Symptoms

These bubbles are visible under the skin and can be found anywhere on the body or the tail. If these gas bubbles are numerous and / or large, they will cause problems with movement and buoyancy.

More dangerous still is the degree of stress the seahorse experiences because of the discomfort and inability to swim as normal. The sick seahorse may stop eating and will die.

Treatment

Bathing the seahorse in a solution containing a medication such as Diamox is effective. However, it is essential to find out what caused the bubbles in the first place or the condition will recur and other seahorses will be affected.

F) Endoparasites (Internal Parasites)

As the name indicates, this condition is caused by internal parasites such as flukes, roundworms, protozoans, flatworms or tapeworms. Fortunately, internal parasites rarely occur in seahorses.

Symptoms

The primary symptom is marked weight loss. In the case of very severe infestations, the parasite may be seen protruding from the anus. These parasites live in the digestive tract and rob the seahorse host of vital nutrients. If untreated, the seahorse will become malnourished and will die.

Treatment

As with the treatment for external parasites, dead shrimp must be injected with an appropriate anti-worming medication such as metronidazole. These shrimp must be fed to the seahorse.

G) *Cryptocaryon irritans*

Cryptocaryon is more commonly known as White Spot Disease or Marine Ichthyophthirius (Ich). It is caused by a protozoan (a single celled organism) called *Cryptocaryon irritans,* which infests fish by burrowing into their skin and later the gills and forming cysts.

It is not a rapidly progressing illness and if it is detected early it can be very successfully treated. However, if it is neglected, the consequences are very serious and can destroy an entire fish population and infest the entire tank.

The life cycle of Cryptocaryon irritans

The life cycle of this protozoan is significant both in terms of the effect on the infected seahorse and why it poses such a huge risk to all the fish in a tank.

The earliest stage of the life of *Cryptocaryon irritans* is when the immature cells, called tomites, are released when the cyst in the host bursts. These tomites float in the water until they find a new host and attach themselves to it.

The next stage in the life cycle is that of a parasitic trophont. These nasty organisms burrow into the flesh or gills of the host and begin to feed on the tissue at that site. Once the trophont has consumed enough, it forms a cyst. These are called inactive tomonts.

Within 6 to 10 days the cells inside the cysts reproduce. Each one becomes a tomite. When the cyst is mature, it ruptures and releases hundreds of tomites into the water. Each one will search for a host.

In other words, the cycle repeats itself and the only difference is that each time there are more tomites. It is easy to see how easily an entire tank can become infected.

Symptoms

The first sign of White Spot Disease or Marine Ich is very small white spots on the fins and body of the seahorse that is host to *Cryptocaryon irritans*. These spots can be as small as grains of salt, which is why a tank owner must be vigilant and observe and monitor fish regularly. This protozoan only moves from the skin to the gills when it has reached the parasitic trophont stage.

Infected seahorses will also rub themselves against objects in the tank. This is an effort to dislodge the parasites on their skin. When the parasites have attacked the fish's gills, the symptoms become far more marked and severe. The gills become blocked by mucous, tissue debris and the tomonts themselves. This results in laboured breathing.

At this advanced stage the fish will have stopped eating, will be very listless and have lost colour in the places where the trophonts destroyed pigment cells in the skin.

There will also be lesions or wounds in the skin, which then become infected by other bacteria.

Treatment of Marine Ich

Treatment needs to be effective for each stage of the life cycle of the *Cryptocaryon irritans*. Not all treatment options work on more than one stage. For example, copper effectively combats the free-swimming tomites but does nothing to deal with trophonts that have burrowed into tissue. To deal with this advanced stage of the infestation, one needs to use a combination of formalin and freshwater treatments. These are administered over an extended period through baths and dips.

A quarantine tank is essential to deal with this problem. You need to generate vigorous aeration in the tank as part of the treatment. Two containers of different types of treatment water also need to be prepared.

In the first one the water should include a formalin product. It is vital that one follows the directions on the packaging so that the solution is correctly mixed. This is the treatment water. It should also contain another product in addition to the formalin that will counteract the ammonia that is a harmful and inevitable by-product of this treatment process. High levels will cause a condition known as ammonia burn.

If you don't have a formalin treatment product, emergency treatment can be provided in the form of a freshwater bath. It won't cure the infestation but it can give a sick seahorse some relief by flushing some mucous out of the gills and removing some parasites from the skin. This eases breathing and reduces irritation. Place the fish in the hyposalinity dip and then back in the quarantine tank. A suitable formalin solution should be obtained as soon as possible.

The second container should contain water with lowered salinity. Hyposalinity or the lowering of specific gravity to approximately 1.010 ppm won't treat or cure the infestation but it does help to prevent re-infestation. It is also used as a dip for fish that have been in the treatment water. This low salinity water helps to remove dead or weak parasites or mucous from the affected fish.

The treatment process must be handled carefully and accurately, as fish requiring these steps are already very sick – perhaps even dying – and weak.

The first stage is to gently place the infested seahorse into the container containing the formalin treatment product. The sicker the seahorse, the more careful one must be. A seriously infested fish may not be able to tolerate the treatment bath for more than a few minutes, if at all, or may even die during the treatment.

When dealing with such badly affected fish, another option is to dilute the solution further, which may make a longer dip time possible. Less badly affected seahorses can remain in the treatment bath for longer (anything up to an hour).

The stage after the treatment bath is a dip in the second container that contains low salinity water. A very stressed or shocked fish may only cope with a 30 second dip. Less severely affected seahorses can tolerate 1 minute or even 2 minutes. Once this dip is finished, the fish should be returned to the quarantine tank.

Seahorses affected by *Cryptocaryon irritans* should be kept in the quarantine tank for the duration of the life cycle of the protozoan / a minimum of 4 weeks. The treatment will continue as directed by the formalin product manufacturers. It is also recommended that an antibacterial be added to the treatment regimen so that one also deals with secondary bacterial infections.

During the period that you are treating your fish, there should be no fish in the main tank. This will ensure that all the protozoa, at each cycle of their life, die off as they are unable to find fish hosts.

Words of caution

- Don't leave seahorses unattended in the treatment bath or the dip. You need to watch them closely and constantly and remove them immediately if they show signs of distress.

- Formaldehyde is a toxic substance and should be used with caution and due care. It should only be used as directed: for parasite infestations and fungal diseases in seahorses and other fish. It is highly toxic to invertebrates and can be harmful to fish if they are exposed to it too often.

- Ensure that the treatment product you select is effective against *Cryptocaryon,* specifically as some are for other types of Ich but are not effective against this protozoan.

Preventing re-infestation

If you don't eliminate the *Cryptocaryon irritans* from the main tank your seahorses will be re-infested regardless of how effectively you treated the fish themselves. As previously mentioned, the main tank must not house any fish for at least 4 weeks.

Creating hyposalinity in the tank speeds up the *Cryptocaryon's* life cycle, which helps while you dose the tank water. However, one can only use this technique if your tank is a fish only tank or not a reef tank. Hyposalinity is not an option if you have corals and various types of invertebrates. There are various solutions available for reef tanks that can be added to the water to destroy *Cryptocaryon* at each stage of the life cycle.

Before you can reintroduce your fish back into the main tank you must change filtering materials, clean filters very thoroughly and do a full water change. Then run a full battery of tests to ensure that all the water and environmental parameters are correct.

H) Brooklynella

Brooklynella is more commonly known as Clown Fish Disease. However, despite this name, it is not only Clown Fish that become infested, but all fish including seahorses. This disease is another form of Ich and is caused by a protozoan (a single celled organism) called *Brooklynella hostilis,* which infests seahorses and fish by burrowing into their skin and later the gills and forms cysts.

Brooklynella, unlike *Cryptocaryon,* is a very rapidly progressing illness and can kill a seahorse with frightening speed: within a few hours or days. This means that immediate diagnosis and quick treatment is essential to prevent the loss of all the fish in the tank.

Symptoms

The signs and symptoms of this aggressive disease are dramatic and distressing to see. *Brooklynella,* again unlike *Cryptocaryon,* attacks the gills first. In its efforts to dislodge the parasite, a fish will scrape against rocks, corals or other hard surfaces.

As the gills become increasingly affected, seahorses begin to breathe rapidly and will gasp for air. This inability to breathe is due to a build-up of thick mucous that clogs the gills. Hardly surprisingly, fish with *Brooklynella* stop eating, their colour fades, they become very lethargic, and they develop lesions on their skin. These lesions in turn often become infected.

Treatment

Treatment recommendations include a solution of malachite green or copper sulphate used in conjunction with formaldehyde. However, many aquarists believe the most effective treatment for *Brooklynella* is formaldehyde used on its own along with a hyposalinity dip. Treatment should be administered over an extended period.

A quarantine tank is essential to deal with this problem. You need to generate vigorous aeration in the tank as part of the treatment. Two containers of different types of treatment water also need to be prepared.

In the first one, the water should include a formalin product. It is vital that one follows the directions on the packaging so that the solution is correctly mixed. This is the treatment water. It should also contain another product in addition to the formalin that will counteract the ammonia that is a harmful and inevitable by-product of this treatment process. High levels will cause a condition known as ammonia burn.

If you don't have a formalin treatment product, emergency treatment can be provided in the form of a freshwater bath. It won't cure the infestation but it can give a sick seahorse some relief by flushing some mucous out of the gills and removing some parasites from the skin. This eases breathing and reduces irritation. Place the fish in the hyposalinity dip and then back in the quarantine tank. A suitable formalin solution should be obtained as soon as possible.

The second container should contain water with lowered salinity. Hyposalinity or the lowering of specific gravity to approximately 1.010 ppm won't treat or cure the infestation but it does help to prevent re-infestation. It is also used as a dip for fish that have been in the treatment water. This low salinity water helps to remove dead or weak parasites and some mucous from the affected fish.

The treatment process must be handled carefully and accurately, as seahorse requiring these steps are already very sick – perhaps even dying – and weak.

The first stage is to gently place the infested seahorse into the container containing the formalin treatment product. The sicker it is the more careful one must be. A seriously infested fish may not be able to tolerate the treatment bath for more than a few minutes, if at all, or may even die during the treatment.

When dealing with such sick and weak seahorses, another option is to dilute the solution further, which may make a longer dip time possible. Less badly affected fish can remain in the treatment bath longer (anything up to an hour).

The stage after the treatment bath is a dip in the second container that contains low salinity water. A very stressed or shocked fish may only cope with a 30 second dip. Less severely affected fish can tolerate 1 minute or even 2 minutes. Once this dip is finished, the seahorse should be returned to the quarantine tank.

Fish affected by *Brooklynella* should be kept in the quarantine tank for the duration of the life cycle of the protozoan or at least 4 weeks. The treatment will continue as directed by the formalin product manufacturers. It is also strongly recommended that an antibacterial be added to the treatment regimen so that one also deals with secondary bacterial infections.

During the period that you are treating your fish there should be no fish in the main tank. This will ensure that all the protozoan, at each cycle of their life, die off as they are unable to find fish hosts.

Words of caution

- Don't leave seahorses unattended in the treatment bath or the dip. You need to watch them closely and constantly and remove them immediately if they show signs of distress.

- Formaldehyde is a toxic substance and should be used with caution and due care. It should only be used as directed, for parasite infestations and fungal diseases in fish. It is highly toxic to invertebrates and can be harmful to fish if they are exposed to it too often.

- Ensure that the treatment product you select is effective against *Brooklynella* specifically as some are for other types of Ich but are not effective against this protozoan.

I) Oodinium

Oodinium, also known as Velvet Disease or Coral Fish Disease, is caused by a dinoflagellate (a protist or parasitic, single-celled microorganism) called *Amyloodinium ocellatum*. This nasty type of infestation is another of the Ich diseases.

Amyloodinium, like *Brooklynella*, is a very rapidly progressing illness and can kill a seahorse within a few hours or days. This organism also reproduces very quickly. This means that immediate diagnosis and treatment is essential to prevent the loss of all the seahorses and other fish in the tank.

Symptoms

The symptoms of *Amyloodinium* are very similar to those of *Brooklynella* infestation and this organism also attacks the gills first.

An infected fish will scrape against rocks, corals or other hard surfaces in an effort to dislodge the parasites. As the gills become increasingly affected, fish begin to breathe rapidly and will gasp for air. This inability to breathe is due to a build-up of mucous that clogs the gills. The fish will stop eating, their colour fades and they become very lethargic.

Unlike with *Cryptocaryon*, *Amyloodinium* starts in the gills and then spreads to the body. Tiny cysts on the fish's body and fins become visible. They look like grains of salt and resemble the first sign of White Spot Disease / Marine Ich or *Cryptocaryon*.

What is different, however, is that these cysts at this advanced stage of the disease give the seahorse a tan or golden colouring and a velvet-like film coats the whole fish, which is what gives rise to the name Velvet Disease. The eyes will also cloud over in the final stage of the disease.

The life cycle of Amyloodinium or Oodinium

Like *Cryptocaryon, Amyloodinium ocellatum* has 3 stages in its life cycle.

The first stage in the life cycle is when free-swimming cells, called dinospores, are released when a mature cyst in the host bursts. These dinospores float in the water until they find a new host and they can survive for up to 8 days without a host. Some strains can survive for a month in cooler water.

In the next stage of the life cycle the dinospores loose their ability to swim. They become parasitic trophozoites, which attach to their host by means of a feeding filament. They attack the gill tissue of the seahorse and begin to feed on it. The trophozoite will feed off its host for 3 to 7 days, at which point they are mature. They may drop off the host or stay buried in the host's flesh. The trophozoites remaining in the seahorse form cysts.

At the encysted stage, the organism is called a tomont. Within 5 days the cells inside the cysts reproduce. When the cyst is mature, it ruptures and releases hundreds of tomites or dinospores into the water. Each one will search for a host.

The life cycle then repeats and the only difference is that each time there are more free-swimming dinospores. An entire tank can become infected very quickly.

Treatment

Treatment needs to be effective for each stage of the life cycle of the *Amyloodinium*. Not all treatment options work on more than one stage. To deal with the advanced stage of the infestation one needs to use a combination of treatments. These are administered over an extended period through baths and dips.

A quarantine tank is essential to deal with this problem. Two containers of different types of treatment water also need to be prepared. *Amyloodinium* can survive a broad salinity range (anything from 3 to 45 ppm). As a result, a hyposalinity dip or bath is not at all effective against this parasite.

In the first container the water should include a formalin or formalin and copper solution product. It is vital that one follows the directions on the packaging so that the solution is correctly mixed. This is the treatment water. It should also contain another product in addition to the formalin that will counteract the ammonia, which is a harmful and inevitable by-product of this treatment process. High levels will cause a condition known as ammonia burn.

If you don't have a treatment product, emergency treatment can be provided in the form of a freshwater bath. It won't cure the infestation but it can give a sick fish some relief. A suitable treatment solution should be obtained as soon as possible.

The second container should contain a freshwater dip. This water should have a slightly reduced pH and a specific gravity of 1.001. Some aquarists also add the compound known as Methylene Blue.

The first stage is to place the infected fish into the treatment water. The sicker the seahorse, the more careful one must be. A severely infested fish may not be able to tolerate the treatment bath for more than a few minutes, if at all, or may even die during the treatment.

When dealing with such badly affected fish, another option is to dilute the solution further, which may make a longer dip time possible. Less badly affected seahorses may be able to remain in the treatment bath longer (anything up to an hour).

The stage after the treatment bath is a dip in the second container that holds the fresh water solution as described above. An effective duration for the dip is between 3 and 5 minutes. Don't worry if a fish appears dead and even 'lies down'. This behaviour is a normal initial reaction to being in the fresh water solution. After a minute or two the fish should perk up significantly.

There are two reasons why a freshwater solution is so effective against this parasite. The first is that with *Amyloodinium* the cysts are not as deeply embedded as they are in cases of *Cryptocaryon*. Secondly, the membrane of the cells of the Oodinium cyst isn't strong enough to withstand the change in osmotic pressure caused by a move to fresh water.

As a result of this pressure, the cysts burst. However, in order to achieve this, the fish must remain in the dip for 3 minutes. Once this dip is finished, the seahorse should be returned to the quarantine tank.

Fish affected by *Amyloodinium* should be kept in the quarantine tank for the duration of the life cycle of the parasite. The treatment will continue as directed by the treatment product manufacturers. It is also recommended that an antibacterial be added to the treatment regimen so that one also deals with secondary bacterial infections.

During the period that you are treating your fish, there should be no fish in the main tank. This will ensure that all the dinospores and cysts in the tank die.

Preventing re-infection

If you don't eliminate *Amyloodinium* from the main tank, your seahorses will be re-infested regardless of how effectively you treated the fish themselves. As previously mentioned, the main tank must not house any fish for at least 4 weeks.

Raising the tank temperature to 85 or even 90° Fahrenheit or 29.5 to 32° Celsius will speed up the life cycle. There are also various solutions available for reef tanks that can be added to the water to destroy *Amyloodinium* dinospores.

Before you can reintroduce your fish back into the main tank you must change filtering materials, clean filters very thoroughly and do a full water change. Then run a full battery of tests to ensure that all the water and environmental parameters are correct.

Words of caution

- Don't leave seahorses unattended in the treatment bath or the dip. You need to watch them closely and constantly and remove them immediately if they show signs of distress.

- Formaldehyde is a toxic substance and should be used with caution and due care. It should only be used as directed, for parasite infestations and fungal diseases in fish. It is highly toxic to invertebrates and can be harmful to fish if they are exposed to it too often.

- Ensure that the treatment product you select is effective against *Amyloodinium,* specifically as some are for other types of Ich but are not effective against this parasite.

J) Fin Rot

Fin Rot is thought to be caused by injuries such as nipping by other fish, poor tank conditions or a bacterial infection following injury. They can also be a secondary condition caused by Fish Tuberculosis.

Symptoms

The signs and symptoms of Fin or Tail Rot are easy to spot. The fins look frayed and show signs of disintegration. In very severe cases the fins can be reduced to stumps because the tissue has broken down entirely.

Other signs are bleeding along the edges of the fins, red or inflamed-looking areas at the base of the fin, exposed fin rays (the soft, flexible 'rods' that run the length of the fin) and ulcers on the skin. In seahorses with advanced Rot, their eyes also become cloudy.

Treatment

Given that there are several possible causes of Fin Rot, the first steps must be to establish the cause and place the affected seahorse in a quarantine tank. Once the cause has been determined one must remedy it if possible and treat the fish or the water. For example, if the damage is due to attacks by another fish, you will have to take steps to keep them apart, or if water quality is poor that must be remedied immediately.

Regardless of the cause, you will probably have to use an antibiotic treatment; even if the Rot is not bacterial in origin, the damaged tissue will almost certainly be infected. The choice one has at this point is to either dose the seahorse or the water.

If an antibiotic is added to the water is it very important that the instructions are carefully followed with regards to dosage. In addition, be very cautious about adding medications to a main tank, as they may adversely affect invertebrates and corals.

Your local marine specialist or vet will be able to offer advice as to which antibiotic would be most suitable and to suggest an appropriate dose. Chloromycetin and tetracyclines are quite often used in very small quantities.

K) Gill and Fin Flukes

These flukes are small, worm-like parasites that multiply very quickly. This is a highly infectious disease that is fatal if affected seahorses are not treated very quickly. What makes this parasite so dangerous is that they can clog the gills of the fish, which causes them to suffocate slowly.

Symptoms

As with other parasitic infestations, the affected fish will swim erratically and rub against hard surfaces as they try to dislodge the parasites. Seahorses with these flukes also exhibit rapid and laboured breathing and often have white patches on their bodies and cloudy eyes.

In severe cases the worm-like parasites may sometimes be visible as thin, thread-like objects.

Treatment

A freshwater bath usually kills the majority of the parasites and brings the fish immediate relief from many of the symptoms. For fish that are more severely affected, a longer treatment bath of salt water and methylene blue may be required.

Prevention

Placing new seahorses in a freshwater dip and then keeping them in a quarantine tank for a few weeks before introducing them to the main tank is one of the primary ways to ensure that this parasite is not introduced into your tank.

In addition, ensuring that the water quality is good at all times and that the other environmental parameters in the tank are always as they should be will prevent stress in the tank inhabitants. Stress affects all fish badly, as it damages their mucous coating. Weaknesses in this coating make the fish vulnerable, as parasites can gain hold far more easily.

Finally, the use of a correctly installed ultraviolet (UV) sterilizer will also help to prevent outbreaks of this parasite.

L) Popeye

Popeye is a condition rather than a disease. It is also known as Exopthalmia or Exophthalmos and can be caused by eye trauma or by fungal or bacterial infection / disease.

Trauma can be the result of a scrape, bump or a scratch. Seahorses can injure themselves on objects in the tank, get hurt during fights with other fish, and tank owners can accidentally damage fish's eyes when using an aquarium net. In the case of trauma, it is usually only one eye that is affected. An eye injury can look alarming but often doesn't impact on the overall health of the seahorse.

In the case of infections of some kind, the fish can be far more badly affected in terms of its general health and its ability and desire to feed. Both eyes may also be affected.

The third possible cause of eye problems, including eye infections, is a range of environmental factors:

- Poor water quality
- Contaminated items are introduced into the tank
- The water temperature is too high
- The levels of harmful compounds such as nitrates are above acceptable parameters
- The fish are stressed
- The fish are receiving poor or inadequate nutrition.

Symptoms

Popeye makes the eye look as though it is under pressure and bulging or about to pop out of the socket. Some conditions also make the eye look clouded or opaque.

Treatment for trauma-induced Popeye

The affected seahorse poses no risk to the others in the main tank, as it is not infectious. Handling the seahorse will probably only worsen the injury. However, if the trauma is due to bullying by another fish the bully must be removed. In addition, if the injury is severe the fish must be placed in the quarantine tank for treatment.

Minor injuries will heal on their own over time, but treatment is required for more serious injuries. Aquarists recommend the use of a broad-spectrum antibiotic that is mixed into flake food. This will combat any infection that may start in the wound. Using a liquid vitamin is also suggested and your vet or retailer will be able to advise you on the most appropriate products to use. Eventually the eye will return to normal size.

However, with more serious injuries or where treatment has not been effective, the seahorse may suffer very significant permanent effects. The fish may loose their sight in the affected eye. In this situation the eye will look grey, opaque or even completely colourless.

With very severe eye injuries that go untreated, or where the treatment was not effective, the eye may disappear or burst. The shock and trauma of this can be fatal.

If both eyes are affected and the seahorse looses or partially looses its vision, it will be unable to feed properly and will not survive. Many tank owners prefer to use euthanasia rather than leave a blind fish to slowly and painfully starve to death.

Treatment for infection or disease-induced Popeye

Popeye can also be a symptom, or one of the symptoms, of an underlying medical condition such as an internal fungal or bacterial infection such as *Vibriosis* or kidney disease. In these situations, both eyes are likely to be affected.

If the Popeye is treated rather than the underlying illness *and* the Popeye, then the eye condition naturally won't improve and the fish may die of the underlying medical issue or complications caused by it.

A seahorse with infection or disease-related Popeye must be removed from the general population and placed in a quarantine tank for treatment. Once in 'hospital', both medical issues can be dealt with.

If eye problems can be attributed to poor water quality, 5 to 10% of the tank water must be changed daily. The water must be tested regularly and steps taken to correct any problems. This routine must be continued until the eye conditions have cleared.

M) Ammonia Poisoning and Ammonia Burn

As the name implies, these are not illnesses or diseases but medical conditions caused by levels of ammonia in tank water that are far too high.

These elevated levels are usually due to equipment malfunction or failure, loss of power, when too many new marine creatures are introduced at one time and filters can't cope or when healthy bacteria in the tank have been lost as a result of medications in the water or sudden changes to water parameters.

Symptoms

With ammonia poisoning, the seahorse's gills become red and inflamed. Breathing is difficult and it will gasp for air. Badly poisoned fish loose their appetites and become lethargic. Clamped fins may also be a symptom.

In the advanced stages of poisoning red streaks and patches appear on the skin and fins. These begin to bleed, as do the gills. As tissues are further broken down, the fish begins to haemorrhage internally too and also suffers damage to the central nervous system. Seahorses suffering from ammonia poisoning will die if it is not treated very early.

With ammonia burn there is redness and inflammation on the fins and tail.

Treatment

Treatment involves replacing 25 to 50 % of the water in the aquarium. In addition, the pH must be lowered so that the level is below 7.0.

Seahorses that have been very badly poisoned can't be treated and will die. Euthanasia is a kinder option.

Prevention

The best methods to prevent ammonia poisoning and burn are to test the water regularly, avoid overcrowding in the tank, do regular water changes and make sure that all the essential equipment is working at all times. By doing these things your seahorses won't become victims of this destructive chemical compound.

N) Nitrite / Nitrate Poisoning

Nitrate or Nitrite poisoning is also called Brown Blood Disease. This is not a disease but a serious and potentially fatal medical condition caused by fish being affected / poisoned by elevated levels of nitrates in the water.

One of the lead causes of Nitrate / Nitrite poisoning is a bio-load that is far heavier than the filtration and other tank systems can cope with or following a failure of the filtration system or a prolonged power loss.

Symptoms

There is a range of symptoms that will assist a tank owner to diagnose this form of poisoning in seahorses even if testing the nitrate levels in the tank is not enough to indicate this.

The milder symptoms include lethargy and very limited movement. Poisoned seahorses gasp for air and the gills move very rapidly and loose their normal pink or red colour and turn brown.

The name Brown Blood Disease stems from the increase in levels of methaemoglobin in the blood, which literally turns it brown. It also results in damage to, and loss of, blood cells and organ damage too.

The even more serious aspect of this rise in methaemoglobin is that the seahorse's blood becomes unable to transport oxygen. They and other fish suffering from this condition in effect suffocate to death.

Treatment

The single most important intervention is an immediate water change. Nitrate levels must be tested and watched very closely. Further partial water changes must be done as necessary. In fact, more water changes are necessary the larger the population of the tank.

One also needs to increase the rate of aeration and add chlorine salt (ideally) or aquarium salt to the water. If the affected seahorses are not eating well or at all you must reduce the amount of food you put in the tank. Uneaten food will add to the problems. This regimen must be continued until you get nitrate readings of zero.

Prevention

Performing the necessary routine maintenance, not over feeding or overstocking and testing nitrate levels regularly are the very best ways to prevent a lethal build-up of this toxic compound in the tank water.

In the case of a new tank, the stock should be introduced slowly so that the systems can adjust and accommodate them and toxic compounds such as nitrates don't begin to build up. Levels should be tested regularly.

A red flag for nitrate level problems is an increase in ammonia levels. If your tests pick up raised ammonia there is every chance that, unless you take immediate corrective steps, a nitrate increase will follow very soon.

O) Oxygen Starvation

This condition results from insufficient oxygen due to inadequate water aeration or gas exchange at the surface of the water.

Symptoms

The main symptom is that affected seahorses will gasp for air and the gills move very quickly.

Treatment

The most obvious 'fix' is to increase the levels of aeration, and therefore oxygen, in the tank by increasing airflow and the speed of water circulation through the filters.

Aquarists also suggest that one checks the water temperature. If the temperature goes up, the oxygen requirements go up too. If you find that the water is too warm, it is vital to bring it down to normal levels as quickly as possible. Using the cooling or chilling methods described in an earlier chapter will prove useful and will bring relief to the fish as oxygen becomes available in the water once more.

3) A seahorse First Aid Kit

While one can't prepare for every eventuality, it is a good idea to keep a first aid kit on hand so you can treat your seahorse and other marine creatures immediately if the need arises. Some illnesses are so aggressive that waiting for your vet or a shop to open the next day or Monday morning is simply not an option!

A seahorse First Aid Kit could contain:

- A syringe (without a needle)
- Thin IV catheter flexible tubing (without needle)
- Medications:
  o Formalin solution (37%)
  o Methylene Blue
  o Triple Sulpha
  o Acetazolamide (Diamox)
  o Metronidazole
  o Fenbendazole (Pancur)
  o Doxycycline (Vibramycin)
  o Neomycin
  o Kanamycin
  o Ceftazime (Fortran)
  o Praziquantel (Droncit)
  o Furan 2

A marine tank First Aid Kit should include the following items:

- A refractometer
- Measuring equipment such as syringes and / or pipettes
- A copper test kit
- Medications:

o A copper-based product
o Malachite Green
o An antibacterial agent
o A deworming agent.

There is a range of these products available. Your vet or a specialist retailer will be able to advise you as to which would be best for your tank and requirements.

It's important to check the contents of the kit regularly to make sure that none of the medications or solutions are past their expiry dates. If they are they must be replaced immediately. In addition, as you finish something, you need to purchase more. You don't want to discover you have run out of a life-saving item at the time you really need it!

A quarantine tank is of course a very big part of a tank owner's ability to prevent health problems and deal effectively with them when, not if, they do occur.

4) Pet insurance

If you use a quarantine tank, follow good maintenance routines and schedules to ensure high quality water, and use high quality foods to strengthen immunity, your seahorses and other tank inhabitants should stay pretty healthy. However, marine fish are prone to illness and even the healthiest marine creature can be injured.

Enter pet insurance. It used to be that pet insurance only catered for dogs and cats. In a very recent development there are now some insurers that will cover fish. One would have to establish which companies offer this option and whether it covers seahorses, which are known to be hard to care for!

Chapter 12: Breeding seahorses

Some breeders say that if you want to breed your seahorses you need a bonded pair. However, one can just buy a male and female and in all probability they will pair up!

Once you have your breeding pair, there are things you can do to encourage them to breed such as keeping the quality of the water high. How often they produce young will, in large part, depend on which species of seahorse you have in your tank: some species produce three lots of young a month and others only one; some seahorses breed all year and others only during summer.

The most extraordinary aspect of seahorse reproduction is that it is the male that becomes pregnant and gives birth!

1) Sexual maturity

Seahorses reach physical and sexual maturity before they are fully grown. The way one can tell that a seahorse, regardless of species, is mature is when it is easy to see whether it is male or female.

It's not a good idea to buy an immature seahorse, so if one buys from a reputable breeder the seahorse will be ready to bond and mate.

2) Seahorse dads

There is a lot to be said for the view that male seahorses are the best fathers in the animal kingdom. The reason is that it is the male that gets pregnant, carries the young and then gives birth!

The female deposits her eggs into a special Kangaroo-like pouch, called the brood pouch, which is located at the base of the male's tail. He carries the embryos until they are ready and then, under cover of dark, he gives birth to sometimes hundreds of tiny but fully formed young.

3) Reproduction: courtship and mating

The courtship process and rituals of the seahorse are enchanting, with both male and female taking an active part in it.

The courtship process lasts several days. Some researchers think that this period allows the male and female to synchronize their reproductive states so they are ready to mate at the same time. It can take up to three days for the female's eggs to ripen. The pair remains together throughout this courtship period.

During courtship, the bonded pair swims side-by-side, often holding tails. Several species change colour and become brighter during this time. Before dawn each day the pair 'dances' together by using their tails to grip onto the same hitching post and then wheel around together like horses on a merry-go-round.

The final courtship dance lasts anything up to 8 hours. The male pumps water into his brood pouch and opens it to show that it is empty and ready to receive eggs. When the female's eggs are ready she signals readiness to the male by 'standing' on the tip or point of her tail. The pair let go of their hitching post and drift, snout-to-snout and often in a gentler spiral motion, to the surface of the water.

The female inserts her ovipositor into the male's pouch where she deposits anything from dozens to thousands of eggs depending on the seahorse species. As her body slims the male's swells as his brood pouch fills with eggs. The pair gently moves apart and he seals the pouch opening and sways gently to settle the eggs. He then fertilises them.

Both seahorses then sink slowly to the bottom. Neither will mate again for the duration of the pregnancy.

4) Gestation and birth

The brood pouch provides the eggs with a controlled environment and a supply of oxygen. The eggs hatch in the pouch and the embryos develop in a regulated salt-water environment that prepares them for the water outside.

Depending on species and the water temperature, gestation or pregnancy periods last from 2 weeks to a month (the warmer the water, the shorter the time).

During the pregnancy, the female visits her mate every morning. The greet each other and stay together for 5 or 6 minutes, hitched side-by-side or swimming together. They may also change colour as they do during initial courtship. She then leaves and he continues to feed.

The other contribution from the female is that she deposits far more eggs into the brood pouch than her mate can fertilize. These excess eggs are absorbed by the male's body and provide him with extra nutrients during this demanding time.

The male usually goes into labour at night, as darkness provides him and the babies some protection. The male pumps and thrusts for hours or even days in order to give birth to his offspring.

The babies are tiny and measure between 7 and 12 millimetres or just over ¼ of an inch. They are perfect replicas of their parents and are born independent and free-swimming. As soon as they are born, they rise to the surface of the water and gulp for air. They are immediately able to feed on plankton and grasp with their tails. They will drift away on ocean currents and find their own territory.

The survival rate for seahorses is estimated at 0.5%, which is in fact higher than most fish species. It does help to explain the very high number of offspring they produce.

5) *What you need for babies*

The first thing to point out is that raising seahorse young is not easy at all; even experienced aquarists find it difficult. If breeding seahorses is why you want to buy them… think again!

The first item you must have is a nursery tank. It only needs to be a small (5 gallons or 22.5 UK litres or 17.5 US litres) tank, although you can use a larger one if you choose to do so. These tanks, like quarantine tanks, can be sparse in terms of equipment. All that is necessary is a heater or heating mat and an air pump. The air bubbles should be slow with airlines in the corners of the tank.

There is no need for substrate or any tank décor other than suitably sized hitching posts such as nylon or thin plastic string. Lighting is also not needed if there is sufficient ambient light in the room the tank is in. However, a light to the side of the tank helps to make the tiny babies more visible.

What is essential is that the pH level and temperature of the water are as close to those in the main tank as possible. Some aquarists recommend that one exchange half of the fresh water from the nursery tank with that of the main aquarium so that the water conditions are as close as possible.

In the event that the male gives birth in the main tank, you will have to remove the babies. The first important step is to turn off all the pumps and filters in the main tank. It's important that there is no current or flow and no risk that these tiny young seahorses could be sucked into filter or skimmer pipes etc.

The nursery tank must be kept clean, as babies are even more susceptible to bacterial infections than adult seahorses. One must vacuum the bottom of the tank daily to remove uneaten food and faecal matter. It is also necessary to change 50% of the water each day and wipe down the surfaces every few days in order to remove algae.

As with any tank, pH, temperature, ammonia and nitrite levels must be checked daily. With so many little fish being fed a lot of food, water quality can go badly wrong very fast.

6) Unexpected babies

If you did not know that you were an expectant 'parent' and discover that you have a tank full of tiny baby seahorses, you need to act as soon as possible.

Your first step must be to switch of pumps and filters, as these could injure or kill baby seahorses. You then need to very, very carefully catch and remove them from the main tank. Use a cup or glass and never a net, as they can injure the babies. In addition, they should never be exposed to air! Seahorse fry are attracted to light, so you could use light to 'herd' and then gather them.

Place them in a container such as a large bowl or bucket until you have a nursery tank. It must, however, not be a container that has ever housed chemicals of any kind. The makeshift nursery must be filled with water from the main tank.

Your next decision is: do you want to raise these tiny creatures? An aquarist needs to be honest and realistic about whether he or she is up for the challenge because it will take time, energy and money and many will die, so it can be heart breaking too.

If you decide you want to care for them, you need to dash out and buy the equipment you need for the nursery tank and suitable food. The young seahorses do have yolk sacs that they feed from. Nevertheless, you only have between 24 and 36 hours after they are born to start feeding them or they will die.

7) Feeding seahorse babies

The ideal food for seahorse fry is baby brine shrimp. Young seahorses must be fed every few hours. The amount provided should mean that there is no food left in the tank by the time of the next feed but that there is enough in the water that the babies, who are still weak, don't have to move too much to feed.

Once the young seahorses are 6 or 8 weeks of age they can move on to chopped, frozen mysis and adult brine shrimp. If some young are not eating the adult shrimp you need to combine them with baby shrimp until all the seahorses can eat the adult brine shrimps.

The addition of mysis unfortunately means dirtier water, so one has to clean the tank more often. However, the lipids in this food are essential for the growing young.

8) Breeding food for fry

Ideally, an aquarist should breed the food that the seahorses need. Doing so can sometimes be as tricky as raising the babies!

Brine Shrimp

One can buy Brine Shrimp hatcheries, most of which consist of a stand and a pipe so that a small aerator can be attached. The final item one needs to use is a two litre (a ½ gallon) plastic bottle or other suitable container. Marine retailers supply packets of Brine Shrimp eggs and salt for inclusion in the water.

The container should be filled to a few inches below the rim. The supplied salt should be mixed into prepared water. Once the aerator hose has been placed into the container, one can simply pour the Brine Shrimp eggs into the water. The eggs will hatch in 24 to 48 hours.

The shells left behind after Brine Shrimp have hatched are brown and they float, often to the surface of the water in the hatchery. The hatched shrimps, on the other hand, stay at the bottom. This makes it much easier to remove the shells, which can't and shouldn't be used as food. The eggs can be skimmed off using a suitable net or a pipette.

The Brine Shrimp that you have grown should only be kept for 3 or 4 few days after they have hatched. This means that you need to place eggs in the hatchery on a staggered basis so that there are always newly hatched shrimp for your seahorse babies to eat.

Chapter 13: Prices, costs & where to buy seahorse

1) Costs

The cost to purchase a seahorse:

These amazing fish do not come cheap! A seahorse will set you back between £26 / $40 and £52 / $80. On top of that you will need to pay for all the equipment you will need before you can even take your new pet home.

Set-up costs:

You need certain basic equipment for your seahorses. These one-off costs include:

- Tank or aquarium: depending on size and design, the prices range from $55 / £37 to $2000 / £1349. Some of these prices include a hood or cover and an under-substrate filter. The very expensive tanks may include housing such as a cabinet and a number of pieces of equipment.
- Substrate: $9 – 39 / £6 – 26
- Live rocks: $22 – 30 / £15 – 20
- Live sand: $34 / £23
- Coral: $4.50 – 33 / £3 – 22
- Algae sheets or attack pack: $3 – 16 / £2 – 11
- Filter: $ 5.50 – 25 / £4 – 17
- Calcium reactor: $190 – 312 / £128 – 211
- Thermometer: $2.75 – 18 / £1.85 – 12
- Powerhead: $22 – 70 / £15 – 47
- Wave makers and oscillators: $176 – 296 / £119 – 200
- Air pump: $12 – 85 / £8 – 57
- Heater: $29 – 38.50 / £ 19 – 26
- Protein skimmer: $89 – 281 / £60 – 190
- Full spectrum light: $6 – 296 / £4 – 200
- Water conditioner: $2 – 13 / £1.35 – 9

- Hydrometer: $9 – 17 / £6 – 11.25
- Refractometer: $12 / £8
- Detritus attack pack: $39 – 160 / £26.30 – 108
- Water test kit: $14.50 – 40 / £10 – 27
- Water filter: $13 – 150 / £8.50 – 101

Optional items include:

- Carbon filtration system: $89 – 218 / £60 – 147.50
- Reverse Osmosis (RO) or Deionization (DI) filtration unit: $123 – 388 / £83 – 262
- UV Steriliser: $16 – 297 / £11 – 200

These are just for a single tank or aquarium. Additional tanks and a few of the most basic items will be necessary for a nursing and a quarantine tank.

You may be able to buy items, including second-hand or pre-owned ones, more cheaply online but then you need to think about how clean these items might be. The last thing you want is to acquire a tank that is infected with bacteria, a virus or a parasite that will infect all your stock.

Ongoing, regular costs:

These expenses include all the items you need for regular, routine maintenance and hygiene and for the overall health and well being of your seahorse and other marine tank inhabitants:

- Aquarium salt mix: $22 – 74 / £15 – 50
- Limewater: $18 – 21 / £12 – 14
- Aquarium nets: $4 – 6 / £3 – 4
- Aquarium brushes: $11 / £7.50
- Marine flake food: $5 – 11 / £3.30 – 7.25
- Krill: $3 / £1.80
- Shrimp or Mysis: $5 – 10 / £3.15 – 7
- Spirulina flakes: $6 / £4.25
- Brine Shrimp eggs: $12 – 16 / £8 – 10.80

These regular costs obviously don't include any emergencies or unforeseen 'extras' that you may encounter such as vet bills for tests, for example.

2) *Where you can buy seahorses*

Buying equipment from more general or non-specialist retailers is usually fine. However, one needs to be careful about where one buys seahorses. Only buy from a reputable retailer!

One doesn't want to obtain specimens that are sold as captive-bred but are in actual fact wild caught or tank-raised. In addition, less specialised retailers may, deliberately or inadvertently, sell seahorses that are close to the end of their life span or sick.

You could ask a vet that includes fish in his or her practise for recommendations about local breeders. In addition, do research on the Internet. Joining seahorse groups, clubs and forums online is a wonderful way to find information.

There are shops that one can visit and a large number of reputable online marine specialist shops where one can buy fish that will be shipped safely.

Chapter 14: Conclusion

1) Do's... in no particular order

- ✓ Learn about seahorse and marine aquarium care

- ✓ Find out what fish and other species are compatible and can share a tank

- ✓ Make sure you get a tank that is large enough

- ✓ Only buy mature seahorses

- ✓ Only buy captive-bred fish rather than wild-caught or tank-raised seahorses

- ✓ Observe seahorses carefully to look for signs of ill health before buying a fish

- ✓ Cure live rocks before placing them in the aquarium

- ✓ Take the time to set up the aquarium or tank properly

- ✓ Include an algae attack pack

- ✓ Make use of a detritus attack pack

- ✓ Invest in good quality tank equipment

- ✓ Buy and equip a smaller tank that will be used as a quarantine or hospital tank (or a nursery tank at a pinch)

- ✓ Ensure that the water quality of always good

- ✓ Draw up a maintenance schedule

- ✓ Perform regular maintenance

- ✓ Check and meet all the necessary water and tank parameters (salinity, pH, temperature, calcium, phosphates, etc.)

✓ Take the time to acclimate all marine creatures using either the float or the drip method before placing them in a tank

✓ Deal with salt creep

✓ Be prepared for a loss of power

✓ Feed seahorses a varied diet

✓ Keep a First Aid Kit.

2) Don'ts… in no particular order

- Use tap water

- Use common table salt

- Fail to test water parameters regularly

- Neglect routine maintenance tasks including performing water replacements

- Introduce uncured live rocks in the aquarium

- Rush the vital acclimation process

- Feed seahorses frozen food that has degenerated

- Over-feed

- Place too many marine creatures in a tank so you have over crowding, which causes stress

- Ignore signs of ill health

- Neglect to make contingency plans for in the event of a power failure

- Leave seahorses unattended in the treatment bath or the dip

- Buy "all-in-one" aquarium kits

- Choose a seahorse based on its colour, as these fish change colour depending on their age, mood and the tank environment

- Buy seahorses that have been housed in a tank with other fish, as they may carry parasites or diseases that seahorses have no resistance to

- Buy seahorses that have been housed with pipefish or dragon fish, as they carry diseases or parasites that seahorses have no resistance to.

3) A reminder of the big mistakes that cost!

One needs to take being a seahorse owner very seriously, because they are not easy to care for and are living creatures. This commitment must begin before you even bring your new pet home. These creatures are entirely dependent on the tank owner, who can't decide to take a few days off or go away without making provision for the care of the aquarium.

An aquarium is a "closed system" and without due care the marine creatures in it will not survive. An aquarist or hobbyist must take the time and trouble to become informed by learning about the species and about caring for marine or saltwater tanks.

The main reason that seahorses die in tanks – as a rule – is because owners are either ignorant or don't care for the inhabitants properly. The primary causes of aquarium fish death are:

Improper or no acclimation

It's not enough to acclimatise new seahorses to water temperature alone because this is just one of the important environmental factors.

They also need to be acclimated to the pH. The shock of a sudden change in pH can kill seahorses, as they are particularly sensitive to this particular parameter.

Incorrect diet or insufficient food

If seahorses, like any other living creature, don't receive enough food, they will become malnourished and weak. Seahorses, however, are affected even faster than many fish species because they have simple, immature digestive systems, which don't allow them to store food.

Malnutrition impacts on the immune systems and seahorses that are weakened in this way are far less likely to be able to fend off or fight an infection or infestation. If there is no food provided, seahorses will starve to death rapidly.

In addition to not being given enough food, being fed the wrong diet is also a big problem. Either seahorses simply won't eat a food item that they are unfamiliar with or can't cope with or they will eat it and be adversely affected by it.

Contamination of the aquarium and stock

Not using a quarantine tank can be disastrous. Seahorses may initially appear healthy, and a retailer may supply specimens in good faith, but they may be carrying parasites, including ones that cause very serious illness such as Cryptocaryon and Oodinium. Not only will the infected fish require treatment, which may or may not be successful, but all the other fish in the tank might become infected.

Using a quarantine tank will usually save your fish from illness and suffering and you from a great deal of work, expense and distress.

Poor water quality

Seahorses must have a stable environment that stays within certain set parameters. These are non-negotiable and include the correct levels or total absence of certain compounds, pH and salinity levels, oxygenation levels and temperature. Temperature and pH are especially vital. Not testing these parameters regularly will prove very costly to you and your seahorses and other marine creatures.

If water is not of high quality, seahorses become stressed and this weakens their immune systems. This leaves them vulnerable to attack by bacteria, viruses and parasites.

Good water quality is not difficult to maintain if one prepares water properly and carries out all of the necessary maintenance tasks, including the very important partial water changes, correctly and regularly. This would also include ensuring that vital equipment such as filters and skimmers are working as they should.

Species incompatibility

Not all seahorse species get on well together. In addition, seahorses are only compatible with specific corals, fish and invertebrates.

Part of the all-important homework that must be done before setting up an aquarium is to examine compatibility so that the residents of your aquarium get on and don't attack each other, get injured or become stressed.

4) And in closing...

This guide's primary purpose is to make sure that you have the information that you need to decide, first and foremost, if this is really the right fish for you, for your spouse, or for your child.

If the answer is a confident and honest "yes", this pet owner's guide will also give you the details that will help you to keep your seahorse healthy and happy.

All animals in captivity should at least live to their usual or expected life span. In fact, given they are safe from their natural predators and receive a good diet and care, they should exceed the average life span for their species. If you are one of those individuals who commits to owning and caring for one of these amazing fish, you will be rewarded by having a pet that is fascinating, beautiful and rewarding! Enjoy your seahorse and teach others about them.

Published by IMB Publishing 2015

Made in the USA
Middletown, DE
22 November 2020